200 Light
chicken dishes

hamlyn | **all colour cookbook**

200 Light
chicken dishes

An Hachette UK Company
www.hachette.co.uk

First published in Great Britain in 2015 by Hamlyn
a division of Octopus Publishing Group Ltd
Endeavour House, 189 Shaftesbury Avenue
London, WC2H 8JY
www.octopusbooks.co.uk

ISBN: 978-0-600-62899-6

A CIP catalogue record for this book is available
from the British Library.

Printed and bound in China

10 9 8 7 6 5 4 3 2 1

Both metric and imperial measurements have
been given in all recipes. Use one set of measurements
only, and not a mixture of both.

Standard level spoon measurements are used in all recipes.
1 tablespoon = one 15 ml spoon
1 teaspoon = one 5 ml spoon

Ovens should be preheated to the specified temperature
– if using a fan-assisted oven, follow the manufacturer's
instructions for adjusting the time and temperature.

Fresh herbs should be used unless otherwise stated.
Medium eggs should be used unless otherwise stated.

The Department of Health advises that eggs should not
be consumed raw. This book contains some dishes made
with raw or lightly cooked eggs. It is prudent for vulnerable
people such as pregnant and nusing mothers, invalids,
the elderly, babies and young children to avoid uncooked
or lightly cooked dishes made with eggs. Once prepared,
these dishes should be kept refrigerated and used promptly.

This book includes dishes made with nuts and nut
derivatives. It is advisable for those with known allergic
reactions to nuts and nut derivatives and those who may
be potentially vulnerable to these allergies to avoid dishes
made with nuts and nut oils. It is also prudent to check the
labels of pre-prepared ingredients for the possible inclusion
of nut derivatives.

contents

introduction

introduction

this series

The Hamlyn All Colour Light Series is a collection of handy-sized books, each packed with over 200 healthy recipes on a variety of topics and cuisines to suit your needs.

The books are designed to help those people who are trying to lose weight by offering a range of delicious recipes that are low in calories but still high in flavour. The recipes show a calorie count per portion, so you will know exactly what you are eating. These are recipes for real and delicious food, not ultra-slimming meals, so they will help you maintain your new healthier eating plan for life. They must be used as part of a balanced diet, with the cakes and sweet dishes eaten only as an occasional treat.

how to use this book

All the recipes in this book are clearly marked with the number of calories (kcal) per serving. The chapters cover different calorie bands: under 500 calories, under 400 calories, etc.

There are variations on each recipe at the bottom of the page – note the calorie count as they do vary and can sometimes be more than the original recipe.

The figures assume that you are using low-fat versions of dairy products, so be sure to use skimmed milk and low-fat yogurt. They have also been calculated using lean meat, so make sure you trim meat of all visible fat

and remove the skin from chicken breasts. Use moderate amounts of oil and butter for cooking and low-fat/low-calorie alternatives when you can.

Don't forget to take note of the number of portions each recipe makes and divide up the quantity of food accordingly, so that you know just how many calories you are consuming.

Be careful too, about side dishes and accompaniments that will also add to calorie content.

Above all, enjoy trying out the new flavours and exciting recipes that this book contains. Rather than dwelling on the thought that you are denying yourself your usual unhealthy treats, think of your new regime as a positive step towards a new you. Not only will you

lose weight and feel more confident, but your health will benefit, the condition of your hair and nails will improve, and you will exude a healthy glow.

the risks of obesity

Up to half of women and two-thirds of men are overweight or obese in the developed world today. Being overweight can not only make us unhappy with our appearance, but can also lead to serious health problems, including heart disease, high blood pressure and diabetes.

When someone is obese, it means they are overweight to the point that it could start to seriously threaten their health. In fact, obesity ranks a close second to smoking as a possible cause of cancer. Obese women are more likely to have complications during and after pregnancy, and people who are overweight or obese are also more likely to suffer from coronary heart disease, gallstones, osteoarthritis, high blood pressure and type 2 diabetes.

how can I tell if I am overweight?

The best way to tell if you are overweight is to work out your body mass index (BMI). If using metric measurements, divide your weight in kilograms (kg) by your height in metres (m) squared. (For example, if you are 1.7 m tall and weigh 70 kg, the calculation would be 70 ÷ 2.89 = 24.2.) If using imperial measurements, divide your weight in pounds (lb) by your

height in inches (in) squared and multiply by 703. Then compare the figure to the list below (these figures apply to healthy adults only).

Less than 20	underweight
20–25	healthy
25–30	overweight
Over 30	obese

As we all know by now, one of the major causes of obesity is eating too many calories.

what is a calorie?

Our bodies need energy to stay alive, grow, keep warm and be active. We get the energy we need to survive from the food and drinks we consume – more specifically, from the fat, carbohydrate, protein and alcohol that they contain.

A calorie (cal), as anyone who has ever been on a diet will know, is the unit used to measure how much energy different foods contain. A calorie can be scientifically defined as the energy required to raise the temperature of 1 gram of water from 14.5°C to 15.5°C. A kilocalorie (kcal) is 1,000 calories and it is, in fact, kilocalories that we usually mean when we talk about the calories in different foods.

Different food types contain different numbers of calories. For example, a gram of carbohydrate (starch or sugar) provides 3.75 kcal, protein provides 4 kcal per gram, fat provides 9 kcal per gram and alcohol provides 7 kcal per gram. So, fat is the most concentrated source of energy – weight for weight, it provides just over twice as many calories as either protein or carbohydrate – with alcohol not far behind. The energy content of a food or drink depends on how many grams of carbohydrate, fat, protein and alcohol are present.

how many calories do we need?

The number of calories we need to consume varies from person to person, but your body weight is a clear indication of whether you are eating the right amount. Body weight is simply determined by the number of calories you are eating compared to the number of calories your body is using to maintain itself and needs for physical activity. If you regularly consume more calories than you use up, you will start to gain weight as extra energy is stored in the body as fat.

Based on our relatively inactive modern-day lifestyles, most nutritionists recommend that women should aim to consume around 2,000 calories (kcal) per day, and men an amount of around 2,500. Of course, the amount of energy required depends on your level of activity: the more active you are, the more energy you need to maintain a stable weight.

a healthier lifestyle

To maintain a healthy body weight, we need to expend as much energy as we consume; to lose weight, energy expenditure must therefore exceed intake of calories. So, exercise is a vital tool in the fight to lose weight. Physical activity doesn't just help us control body weight; it also helps to reduce our appetites and is known to have beneficial effects on the heart and blood that help prevent cardiovascular disease.

Many of us claim we don't enjoy exercise and simply don't have the time to fit it into our hectic schedules. So the easiest way to increase physical activity is by incorporating it into our daily routines, perhaps by walking or cycling instead of driving (particularly for short journeys), taking up more active hobbies such as gardening, and taking small and simple steps, such as using the stairs instead of the lift whenever possible.

As a general guide, adults should aim to do at least 30 minutes of moderate-intensity exercise, such as a brisk walk, five times a week. In place of 30 minutes three sessions of 10 minutes are just as beneficial. Children and young people should be encouraged to take at least 60 minutes of moderate-intensity exercise every day.

Some activities will use up more energy than others. The following list shows some examples of the energy a person weighing 60 kg (132 lb) would expend doing the following activities for 30 minutes:

activity	energy
Ironing	69 kcal
Cleaning	75 kcal
Walking	99 kcal
Golf	129 kcal
Fast walking	150 kcal
Cycling	180 kcal
Aerobics	195 kcal
Swimming	195 kcal
Running	300 kcal
Sprinting	405 kcal

make changes for life

The best way to lose weight is to try to adopt healthier eating habits that you can easily maintain all the time, not just when you are trying to slim down. Aim to lose no more than 1 kg (2 lb) per week to ensure you lose only your fat stores. People who go on crash diets lose lean muscle as well as fat and are much more likely to put the weight back on again soon afterwards.

For a woman, the aim is to reduce her daily calorie intake to around 1,500 kcal while she is trying to lose weight, then settle on around 2,000 per day thereafter to maintain her new body weight. Regular exercise will also make a huge difference: the more you can burn, the less you will need to diet.

improve your diet

For most of us, simply adopting a more balanced diet will reduce our calorie intake and lead to weight loss. Follow these simple recommendations:

Eat more starchy foods, such as bread, potatoes, rice and pasta. Assuming these replace the fattier foods you usually eat, and you don't smother them with oil or butter, this will help reduce the amount of fat and increase the amount of fibre in your diet. As a bonus, try to use wholegrain rice, pasta and flour, as the energy from these foods is released more slowly in the body, making you feel fuller for longer.

Eat more fruit and vegetables, aiming for at least five portions of different fruit and vegetables a day (excluding potatoes).

As long as you don't add extra fat to your fruit and vegetables in the form of cream, butter or oil, these changes will help reduce your fat intake and increase the amount of fibre and vitamins you consume.

who said vegetables must be dull?

Eat fewer sugary foods, such as biscuits, cakes and chocolate bars. This will also help reduce your fat intake. If you fancy something sweet, aim for fresh or dried fruit instead.

Reduce the amount of fat in your diet, so you consume fewer calories. Choosing low-fat versions of dairy products, such as skimmed milk and low-fat yogurt, doesn't necessarily mean your food will be tasteless. Low-fat versions are available for most dairy products, including milk, cheese, crème fraîche, yogurt, and even cream and butter.

Choose lean cuts of meat, such as back bacon instead of streaky, and chicken breasts instead of thighs. Trim all visible fat off meat before cooking and avoid frying foods – grill or roast instead. Fish is also naturally low in fat and can make a variety of tempting dishes.

simple steps to reduce your calorie intake

Few of us have an iron will, so when you are trying to cut down make it easier on yourself by following these steps:

- Serve small portions to start with. You may feel satisfied when you have finished, but if you are still hungry you can always go back for more.
- Once you have served up your meal, put away any leftover food before you eat. Don't put heaped serving dishes on the table as you will undoubtedly pick, even if you feel satisfied with what you have already eaten.
- Eat slowly and savour your food; then you are more likely to feel full when you have finished. If you rush a meal, you may still feel hungry afterwards.
- Make an effort with your meals. Just

because you are cutting down doesn't mean your meals have to be low on taste as well as calories. You will feel more satisfied with a meal you have really enjoyed and will be less likely to look for comfort in a bag of crisps or a bar of chocolate.

- Plan your meals in advance to make sure you have all the ingredients you need. Casting around in the cupboards when you are hungry is unlikely to result in a healthy, balanced meal.
- Keep healthy and interesting snacks to hand for those moments when you need something to pep you up. You don't need to succumb to a chocolate bar if there are other tempting treats on offer.

chicken

Chicken is highly versatile, and with 200 recipes to choose from in this book we hope that you will be able to add some new favourites to your family's repertoire.

Much has been made in the media about the welfare of chickens during rearing. For those on a tight budget, battery-farmed chickens may be the only option. Try to use up the leftovers the following day, or use the redundant carcass to make stock, so that a more expensive free-range chicken, even if not organic, is more cost-effective. While organic, free-range chickens may not be for everyone, try to choose whole chickens and chicken joints with labels indicating that the birds have been reared humanely (for more information, consult the RSPCA in the UK or the HSUS in the USA).

hygiene essentials
- Keep raw and cooked chicken separate in the refrigerator so that raw chicken juices cannot drip on to other foods.
- Cover food dishes so that chicken does not dry out.
- Use separate boards and knives for preparing raw and cooked chicken, as well as for preparing meat and vegetables.
- Defrost frozen chicken in the refrigerator, transferring to room temperature for 1–2 hours before cooking.
- Only reheat cooked food once, and make sure it is piping hot all the way through (don't just warm foods, especially if using the microwave).
- Raw chicken that has been defrosted can only be put back in the freezer if it has been cooked and cooled. If taken out of the freezer in a cooked state, it cannot be refrozen.
- Add a small frozen ice pack to lunchboxes, and use an insulated lunchbag so that any cooked chicken stays cold.

how to make chicken stock
Why bother making your own stock? In an age when we are all being advised to cut down on our salt consumption, homemade stock

can be salt-free; it also fits in with our general tendency to recycle all we can. If you haven't got time to make stock now, don't throw the chicken carcass out – just pack it into a plastic bag and freeze it until you do have time. The following recipe makes 1.4 litres (2½ pints).

chicken carcass from a roast or poached
  whole bird
2 litres (3½ pints) **cold water**
1 large **onion**, cut into quarters but still with
  the inner brown layer of skin attached
2 **carrots**, thickly sliced
2 **celery sticks**, thickly sliced
small bunch of **mixed fresh herbs** or a **dried
  bouquet garni**
black peppercorns

Put the chicken carcass into a large saucepan with the measured water, and add the onion, carrots and celery. Flavour with the fresh herbs or bouquet garni and a few black peppercorns, then bring to the boil. Partially cover the top of the pan with a lid, then leave to simmer gently for 2 hours. Strain into a jug and leave to cool. Store in the refrigerator for 2–3 days or freeze in handy-sized plastic containers or well-sealed plastic bags if the carcass had not already been frozen.

preparation

Before use, always rinse chicken well in cold water, drain well and pat dry with kitchen

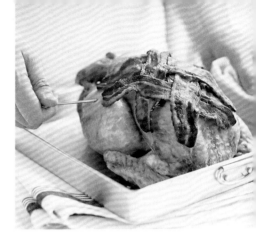

paper; this is especially important if you are using pre-packed raw chicken. When rinsing a whole chicken, take extra care to rinse inside the bird, and remove giblets if included.

If using frozen chicken, make sure it is completely defrosted before use. Don't try to speed up defrosting by plunging it into warm water. Immerse in cold water and change the water frequently, or defrost in the microwave, following the manufacturer's guidelines.

is the chicken cooked?

Chicken must never be served rare or medium, but always well done. Insert a skewer or small knife into the thickest part of a joint, or through a thigh to the breast if cooking a whole chicken. The juices will run clear when the chicken is ready – if you see any traces of pink in the juices, continue cooking. If pan-frying or grilling, check at 5-minute intervals. For a whole chicken, re-test after 15 minutes more in the oven.

how to joint a whole chicken

This is not as tricky as it may first seem; the secret is a good sharp knife and to locate the joints by feel before cutting through them to separate. This technique can be adapted to cut up other poultry too.

1 First remove the trussing strings and put the chicken breast side uppermost on a chopping board. Pull one leg gently away from the body. Cut through the skin between the body and leg, cut down through the meat, and then work down to the thigh joint. Bend the leg so that it eases the leg bone from its socket, then cut through the ball-and-socket joint. Repeat with the other leg.

2 To remove the wings, press one wing against the body of the bird so that both parts of the shoulder are visible. Cut through the skin, then down through the joint to sever. Tuck the wingtip under the shoulder to make a triangular shape joint. Repeat with the other wing.

3 Split the carcass by cutting around and under both breasts with poultry shears or strong kitchen scissors. Cut through the rib cage, so separating the backbone from the breasts. Repeat on the other side.

4 Cut along the centre of the breast with poultry shears, strong kitchen scissors or a sharp knife, then either slide a knife under the breast meat on each side of the bone to release two boneless breast joints or cut straight down between the breast bone with a large cook's knife to give two joints on the bone. For a 'supreme' leave the wing joint attached at step 2, but sever at the first joint so separating wing tips from body.

5 Now separate the leg joint into a drumstick and thigh. Put the joint skin side uppermost, then flex the drumstick slightly so that you can see where the central joint is. Cut through the ball-and-socket joint. Repeat with the other leg.

6 You should now have 2 drumsticks, 2 thigh joints, 2 wings and 2 breast joints, plus a carcass (not pictured) to make stock with. When the bird is small, leave the drumstick and thigh joint joined together.

how to spatchcock a chicken or poussin

Here the bird is split and then flattened so that it cooks more quickly. This enables a whole bird to be barbecued, grilled or roasted traditionally in a shorter time.

1 Put the chicken or poussin breast side

down on a chopping board and remove the trussing string. Cut the bird in half, while keeping the two halves still attached, using poultry shears or sturdy kitchen scissors.

2 Turn the bird over, then using the palm of your hand press down on the breast and flatten it slightly.

3 Trim off the knuckle bones from the drumsticks and tuck the wingtips under the bird. Neaten off any untidy skin and insert two long metal or wooden skewers through each leg, breast and wing so that they cross under the bird and keep it flat during roasting or barbecuing.

how to carve a roast chicken

A good carving knife and fork are essential. Choose a knife that has a long, slightly flexible blade and a fork with tines that are close together. Even more importantly, you must keep the knife sharp. If you find using a knife steel too daunting, there are many hand or electrical knife sharpeners available from good cookshops or major department stores – it really is worth investing in one. Carve off just the amounts you need at a time, working first on one side and then on the other side of the bird, as needed. If the bird is stuffed, don't forget to serve the stuffing with a spoon.

1 Put the chicken on a large chopping board or serving plate with the breast side uppermost. Steadying the joint with a carving fork, cut the skin between the breast and one thigh joint and work downwards

through the meat to the joint. Bend the leg outwards to locate the thigh joint, then cut down through the joint to remove the first leg.

2 To remove the wing on the same side of the chicken, cut down through the corner of the breast to the wing joint. Flex the wing as you did for the leg to locate the joint, then cut down between the joint to remove the wing.

3 Working on the same side of the chicken, make thin diagonal cuts down the breast to slice the meat, using the fork to steady the joint and to help you to remove each slice.

4 Now that the breast has been sliced, separate the thigh and drumstick joints, then cut thin slices of meat off both joints that follow the direction of the bone.

under 200
calories

chicken burgers & tomato salsa

Calories per serving **135**
Serves **4**
Preparation time **15 minutes**,
  plus chilling
Cooking time **10 minutes**

1 **garlic clove**, crushed
3 **spring onions**, finely sliced
1 tablespoon **pesto**
2 tablespoons chopped **mixed
  herbs**, such as parsley,
  tarragon and thyme
375 g (12 oz) **minced chicken**
2 **sun-dried tomatoes**, finely
  chopped
1 teaspoon **olive oil**

Tomato salsa
250 g (8 oz) **cherry tomatoes**,
  quartered
1 **red chilli**, deseeded and
  finely chopped
1 tablespoon chopped **fresh
  coriander**
grated rind and juice of **1 lime**

Mix together all the burger ingredients, except the oil. Divide the mixture into four and form into burgers. Cover and chill for 30 minutes.

Combine all the salsa ingredients in a bowl.

Brush the burgers with the oil and cook under a high grill or on a barbecue for about 3–4 minutes each side until cooked through.

Serve each burger in a bread roll with the tomato salsa and salad leaves.

For chilli and coriander chicken burgers with mango salsa, make the burgers as above. replacing the sundried tomatoes with a finely chopped red chilli (and using coriander pesto in place of the standard pesto). Accompany with a salsa made from 1 large mango, 1 small red onion, 1 red chilli, 2 tbsps coriander, and 2 tbsps mint leaves, all finely chopped and mixed with the juice of one lime and 2 tsps olive oil. **Calories per serving 191**

asian citrus chicken skewers

Calories per serving **143**

Serves **4**

Preparation time **5 minutes,**
   plus marinating

Cooking time **20 minutes**

500 g (1 lb) boneless, skinless
   chicken breasts, cubed

grated rind and juice of 1
   lemon

2 teaspoons **Chinese 5-spice
   powder**

1 tablespoon **dark soy sauce**

mixed vegetables (carrots,
   spring onions, radishes), cut
   into strips, to serve (optional)

Place the chicken, lemon rind and juice, 5-spice powder and soy sauce in a bowl. Stir to combine, cover, then leave to marinate in the refrigerator for at least 1 hour or overnight.

Thread the chicken pieces on to 4 presoaked wooden skewers, pushing them tightly together. Grill for 10 minutes under a preheated moderate grill. Turn the skewers, baste with any remaining marinade, and grill for a further 10 minutes. Serve on a bed of vegetables, if liked.

For piri piri chicken skewers, mix the grated lemon rind and juice with 2 tablespoons olive oil then add 2 teaspoons piri piri seasoning, 2 teaspoons tomato purée and 2 cloves of finely chopped garlic. Add the chicken, marinade then grill as above. **Calories per serving 201**

chicken & vegetable skewers

Calories per serving **149**
Serves **4**
Preparation time **10 minutes**
Cooking time **15 minutes**

4 **chicken thighs**, skinned and
    boned
2 tablespoons **clear honey**
2 tablespoons **mild
    wholegrain mustard**
1 **courgette**, cut into 8 large
    pieces
1 **carrot**, cut into 8 large
    pieces

Cut the chicken thighs into bite-sized pieces and toss in the honey and mustard, setting some aside for serving. Arrange the chicken pieces on a baking sheet and bake in a preheated oven, 180°C (350°F), Gas Mark 4, for 15 minutes until cooked through and lightly golden. Set aside and leave to cool.

Take 8 bamboo skewers and thread with the cooked chicken pieces and the raw vegetables.

Serve with the honey and mustard mixture for drizzling over. The skewers can also be refrigerated for adding to the following day's lunchbox.

For sticky chicken with honey & garlic, mix together 2 tablespoons tomato ketchup, 2 teaspoons runny honey, 2 finely chopped cloves of garlic and 1 tablespoon of sunflower oil. Dip the chicken into the ketchup mixture then cook as above. Thread on to skewers with 1 red pepper, deseeded, cored and cut into chunks and 8 halved cherry tomatoes. **Calories per serving 158**

miso chicken broth

Calories per serving **163**
Serves **4**
Preparation time **10 minutes**
Cooking time **16–18 minutes**

1 tablespoon **sunflower oil**
2 boneless, skinless **chicken breasts**, diced
250 g (8 oz) **cup mushrooms**, sliced
1 **carrot**, cut into thin matchsticks
1.5 cm (¾ inch) piece **root ginger**, grated
2 large pinches **dried crushed red chillies**
2 tablespoons **brown rice miso paste**
4 tablespoons **mirin** or **dry sherry**
2 tablespoons **light soy sauce**
1.2 litres (2 pints) **water**
2 **pak choi**, thinly sliced
4 **spring onions**, thinly sliced
4 tablespoons chopped **fresh coriander**

Heat the oil in a saucepan, add the chicken and fry for 4–5 minutes, stirring until golden. Add the mushrooms and carrot sticks, then the ginger, chillies, miso, mirin or sherry and soy sauce.

Pour on the water and bring to the boil, stirring. Simmer for 10 minutes.

Add the pak choi, spring onions and chopped coriander and cook for 2–3 minutes until the pak choi has just wilted. Spoon into bowls and serve.

For hot & sour chicken soup, fry the chicken in oil as above, add 125 g (4 oz) sliced mushrooms and 1 carrot, cut into matchsticks. Flavour with 2 finely chopped garlic cloves, 3 teaspoons red Thai curry paste, 1 tablespoon Thai fish sauce and 2 tablespoons light soy sauce. Add 1.2 litres (2 pints) chicken stock, bring to the boil and cook for 10 minutes. Add 125 g (4 oz) sliced mini corn cobs, 50 g (2 oz) sliced mangetout, and spring onions and coriander as above. Cook for 2–3 minutes. Ladle into bowls and serve with lime wedges. **Calories per serving 155**

szechuan chicken

Calories per serving **183**
Serves **4**
Preparation time **5 minutes,**
  plus marinating
Cooking time **16–20 minutes**

3 tablespoons **soy sauce**
2 tablespoons **dry sherry**
1 teaspoon **rice vinegar**
3 cm (1¼ inch) piece **root**
  ginger, peeled and finely
  chopped
1 **garlic clove**, crushed
1 tablespoon **Chinese chilli**
  paste
½ teaspoon **Szechuan**
  peppercorns, ground
1 tablespoon **dark sesame oil**
4 x 125 g (4 oz) boneless,
  skinless **chicken breasts**
chopped **fresh coriander**, to
  garnish

To serve (optional)
soba noodles
Stir-fried oyster mushrooms

Mix together all the ingredients except the chicken and coriander in a shallow dish to make the marinade. Add the chicken breasts, coat well with the marinade and leave to marinate at room temperature for 2 hours.

Heat a griddle pan (or ordinary frying pan). Cook the chicken for 8–10 minutes on each side and garnish with coriander. Serve with soba noodles and stir-fried oyster mushrooms, if liked.

For sesame greens with black bean sauce, to accompany the chicken, fry 2 tablespoons sesame seeds in 1 teaspoon sunflower oil until lightly browned. Add 1 tablespoon soy sauce, cover with a lid and take off the heat. When the bubbling subsides, scoop the seeds into a dish. Rinse 400 g (13 oz) spring greens and thickly slice, stir fry in 1 tablespoon oil with 2 cloves finely chopped garlic until just wilted. Mix in 3 tablespoons ready-made black bean sauce. Serve sprinkled with the seeds. **Calories per serving 124**

chicken noodle soup

Calories per serving **191**
Serves **4**
Preparation time **10 minutes**
Cooking time **12 minutes**

1.2 litres (2 pints) **chicken stock**

1 **star anise**

7 cm (3 inch) piece of **cinnamon stick**, broken up

2 **garlic cloves**, finely chopped

2 tablespoons **Thai fish sauce**

8 **coriander roots**, finely chopped

4 teaspoons **light soft brown sugar**

4 teaspoons **light soy sauce**

200 g (7 oz) boneless, skinless **chicken breast**, cut into cubes

125 g (4 oz) **green vegetables**, such as spring cabbage, chard or pak choi, roughly chopped

75 g (3 oz) **bean sprouts**

200 g (7 oz) **straight-to-wok rice noodles**

15 g (½ oz) **fresh coriander**

Put the chicken stock, star anise, cinnamon stick, garlic, fish sauce, coriander roots, sugar and soy sauce into a large saucepan and bring slowly to the boil.

Add the chicken and simmer gently for 4 minutes. Add the green vegetables and bean sprouts and simmer for 2 minutes.

Divide the noodles between 4 bowls, pour over the soup and sprinkle the coriander on top.

For coconut & chicken soup, replace 400 ml (14 fl oz) of the chicken stock with 400 ml (14 fl oz) canned reduced-fat coconut milk. Cook the stock, herbs and spices, sugar and fish and soy sauces, and chicken as above, simmering the green vegetables and bean sprouts for 2 minutes and adding 125 g (4 oz) shredded mangetout for the final 1 minute of cooking for extra crunch. Ladle into warm serving bowls over noodles as above and garnish with fresh coriander. **Calories per serving 266**

chicken minestrone

Calories per serving **197**
Serves **4**
Preparation time **5 minutes**
Cooking time **10 minutes**

400 g (13 oz) can chopped
   tomatoes
600 ml (1 pint) **chicken stock**
125 g (4 oz) cooked **chicken**,
   chopped
1 **courgette**, chopped
125 g (4 oz) **mixed frozen
   vegetables**
70 g (2½ oz) **mini-pasta
   shapes**
1 tablespoon ready-made
   pesto
salt and **pepper**

Put the tomatoes, stock, chicken, courgette and frozen vegetables in a saucepan. Bring to the boil, stirring, then add the pasta shapes and simmer for 5 minutes until the pasta is just tender.

Season with salt and pepper and stir in the pesto just before serving.

For vegetable chicken & rice, put a 400 g (13 oz) can chopped tomatoes in a saucepan with 200 g (7 oz) chopped cooked chicken, 1 chopped courgette, 125 g (4 oz) frozen mixed vegetables and 125 ml (4 fl oz) chicken stock and heat. Simmer for 5 minutes, add 250 g (8 oz) long grain rice and simmer further, stirring occasionally, for 10 minutes or until the rice is cooked, adding a little boiling water if the mixture is too dry. Stir in 125 g (4 oz) baby spinach leaves until just wilted. **Calories per serving 369**

smoked chicken bruschetta

Calories per serving **195**
Serves **4**
Preparation time **10 minutes**
Cooking time **10 minutes**

½ **ciabatta loaf**, cut into 1 cm
   (½ inch) slices
4 teaspoons **olive oil**
1 **garlic clove**, crushed
2 **spring onions**, finely
   chopped
4 **ripe tomatoes**, finely
   chopped
1 tablespoon chopped **basil**
1 tablespoon **balsamic**
   vinegar
1 **smoked cooked chicken**
   breast, torn into small pieces
salt and **pepper**

Place the bread slices on a baking sheet. Mix together
the oil and garlic and brush over the bread. Bake in a
preheated oven, 180°C (350°F), Gas Mark 4, for 10
minutes until crisp.

Meanwhile, mix together the spring onions, tomatoes,
basil and balsamic vinegar. Season with salt and pepper,
then toss in the chicken pieces.

Spoon the tomato mixture on to the toasts to serve.

For smoked chicken toasts, combine the tomato and
spring onion as above and spread over French toast or
ready-made Krisp rolls. Top with sliced smoked chicken
and basil leaves. **Calories per serving 171**

under 300 calories

tandoori chicken salad

Calories per serving **200**
Preparation time **15 minutes**,
   plus marinating
Cooking time **10 minutes**
Serves **4**

200 g (7 oz) natural **yogurt**
2 tablespoons **lemon juice**
½ teaspoon **ground turmeric**
1 teaspoon **garam masala**
1 teaspoon **cumin** seeds,
   roughly crushed
2 tablespoons **tomato purée**
2 **garlic cloves**, finely chopped
2 cm (¾ inch) piece of **fresh
   root ginger**, finely chopped
3 boneless, skinless **chicken
   breasts**, thickly sliced
1 tablespoon **sunflower oil**

Salad
200 g (7 oz) mixed **salad
   leaves**
small bunch of fresh **coriander**
4 tablespoons **lemon juice**

Mix the yogurt, lemon juice, spices, tomato purée, garlic and ginger together in a shallow non-metallic dish. Add the chicken and toss to coat. Cover and chill for 3–4 hours or until required.

When ready to serve, heat the oil in a large frying pan, lift the chicken out of the marinade and add a few pieces at a time to the pan, until all the chicken is in the pan. Cook over a medium heat for 8–10 minutes until the chicken is browned and cooked through.

Meanwhile, toss the salad leaves and coriander with the lemon juice and divide between serving plates. Spoon the chicken on top and serve immediately.

For tandoori chicken skewers, thread 350g (12 oz) chopped chicken breast on to 8 wooden skewers. Place in a large shallow china dish and spoon over the yogurt marinade as above. When ready to serve, lift out of the marinade and cook under a hot grill, turning occasionally until the chicken is cooked through. Serve with salad dressed with lemon juice above. **Calories per serving 185**

chicken & spinach curry

Calories per serving **205
(excluding rice)**
Serves **4**
Preparation time **10 minutes**
Cooking time **25–30 minutes**

1 tablespoon **vegetable oil**
4 boneless, skinless **chicken
breasts**, about 125 g (4 oz)
each, halved lengthways
1 **onion**, sliced
2 **garlic cloves**, chopped
1 **green chilli**, chopped
4 **cardamom pods**, lightly
crushed
1 teaspoon **cumin seeds**
1 teaspoon **dried chilli flakes**
1 teaspoon **ground ginger**
1 teaspoon **ground turmeric**
250 g (8 oz) baby **spinach
leaves**
300 g (10 oz) **tomatoes**,
chopped
150 ml (¼ pint) **low-fat Greek
yogurt**
2 tablespoons chopped fresh
fresh coriander, plus extra
sprigs to garnish
boiled rice, to serve (optional)

Heat the oil in a large frying pan or wok, add the
chicken, onion, garlic and chilli and fry for 4–5 minutes
or until the chicken begins to brown and the onion to
soften. Add the cardamoms, cumin seeds, chilli flakes,
ginger and turmeric and fry for a further 1 minute.

Add the spinach, cover and cook gently until the spinach
wilts, then stir in the tomatoes, re-cover and simmer
for 15 minutes or until the chicken is cooked through,
removing the lid for the last 5 minutes of cooking.

Stir the yogurt and coriander into the curry and
garnished with sprigs of coriander. Serve with boiled
rice, if liked.

devilled chicken

Calories per serving **207**
Serves **4**
Preparation time **10 minutes**
Cooking time **16–20 minutes**

8 small to medium, **boneless
  chicken thighs**
salad leaves, to serve

For the devil sauce
2 tablespoons **Dijon mustard**
6 drops **Tabasco sauce**
2 **garlic cloves**, crushed
1 tablespoon **soy sauce**

Heat a large griddle pan (or ordinary frying pan).
Remove the skin from the chicken thighs, open them
out and trim away any fat.

To make the devil sauce, mix together the mustard,
Tabasco, garlic and soy sauce in a shallow dish.

Dip the trimmed chicken thighs in the devil sauce and
coat each piece well. Place the chicken pieces flat on
the pan and cook for 8–10 minutes on each side.

Serve hot or cold with salad leaves.

For jerk chicken, mix 3 tablespoons jerk marinade (a
ready-made paste) with the grated rind and juice of ½
an orange and 2 finely chopped cloves of garlic. Dip the
chicken in this mixture then cook as above. Serve with
rice or a salad. **Calories per serving 203**

chicken mulligatawny

Calories per serving **208**
  (excluding poppadums)
Serves **6**
Preparation time **15 minutes**
Cooking time **about 1¼ hours**

2 tablespoon **olive oil**
1 **onion**, finely chopped
1 **carrot**, diced
1 **dessert apple**, peeled,
  cored and diced
2 **garlic cloves**, finely chopped
250 g (8 oz) **tomatoes**,
  skinned if liked, roughly
  chopped
4 teaspoons **medium curry
  paste**
50 g (2 oz) **sultanas**
125 g (4 oz) **red lentils**
1.5 litres (2½ pints) **chicken
  stock**
125 g (4 oz) **leftover cooked
  chicken**, cut into shreds
salt and **pepper**
fresh coriander sprigs, to
  garnish
poppadums, to serve
  (optional)

Heat the oil in a saucepan, add the onion and carrot and fry for 5 minutes, stirring until softened and just turning golden around the edges. Stir in the apple, garlic, tomatoes and curry paste and cook for 2 minutes.

Stir in the sultanas, lentils and stock. Season with salt and pepper and bring to the boil, cover and simmer for 1 hour until the lentils are soft. Mash the soup to make a coarse purée. Add the cooked chicken, heat thoroughly then taste and adjust the seasoning if needed. Ladle into bowls and garnish with coriander sprigs. Serve with poppadums, if liked.

For citrus carrot mulligatawny, fry the onion with 500 g (1 lb) diced carrots in 2 tablespoons sunflower oil for 5 minutes. Omit the next five ingredients, then add the red lentils, the grated rind and juice of 1 orange and ½ lemon and 1.5 litres (2½ pints) vegetable stock. Bring to the boil, cover and simmer for 1 hour. Purée until smooth then reheat and adjust seasoning to serve.
Calories per serving 171

chicken tikka sticks & fennel

Calories per serving **256**
Serves **4**
Preparation time **20 minutes,**
  plus marinating and chilling
Cooking time **8–10 minutes**

1 **onion**, finely chopped
½–1 large **red** or **green
  chilli**, deseeded and finely
  chopped (to taste)
5 cm (¾ inch) piece of **fresh
  root ginger**, finely chopped
2 **garlic cloves**, finely chopped
150 g (5 oz) **fat-free natural
  yogurt**
3 teaspoons **mild curry paste**
4 tablespoons chopped **fresh
  coriander**
4 **chicken breasts**, about
  150 g (5 oz) each, cubed

Fennel raita
1 small **fennel bulb**, about
  200 g (7 oz)
200 g (7 oz) **fat-free natural
  yogurt**
3 tablespoons chopped **fresh
  coriander**
salt and **pepper**

Mix the onion, chilli, ginger and garlic together in a shallow china or glass dish. Add the yogurt, curry paste and coriander and mix together.

Add the cubed chicken to the yogurt mixture, mix to coat, cover with clingfilm and chill for at least 2 hours.

Make the raita. Cut the core away from the fennel and finely chop the remainder, including any green tops. Mix the fennel with the yogurt and coriander and season with salt and pepper. Spoon the raita into a serving dish, cover with clingfilm and chill until needed.

Thread the chicken on to 12 skewers and place them on a foil-lined grill rack. Cook under a preheated grill for 8–10 minutes, turning once, or until browned and the chicken is cooked through. Transfer to serving plates and serve with the raita on the side.

For a red pepper & almond chutney, to serve with the skewers instead of the raita, blend 75 g (3 oz) shop-bought roasted peppers in a blender or food processor, with a handful of mint leaves, 1 chopped garlic clove and ½ teaspoon chilli powder. Blend until smooth, then add salt to taste and 1½ tablespoons toasted flaked almonds. Pulse a couple of times to roughly crush the almonds and stir in 1 tablespoon chopped coriander.
Calories per serving 47

oriental chicken cakes

Calories per serving **213**
  (excluding rice noodle
  salad)
Serves **4**
Preparation time **15 minutes**
Cooking time **16 minutes**

575 g (1 lb 3 oz) **minced**
  chicken
1 **stalk lemon grass**, very
  finely chopped
2 **kaffir lime leaves**, very
  finely chopped
5 cm (2 inch) piece **root**
  ginger, peeled, very finely
  chopped
2 **green chillies**, very finely
  chopped
2 **garlic cloves**, very finely
  chopped
1 **egg**, beaten
1 tablespoon **sesame seeds**,
  toasted

To serve
sweet chilli dipping sauce
rice noodle salad with
  chopped **peanuts**, sliced
  onion, **beansprouts** and
  chopped fresh **coriander**
  (optional)

Place the chicken in a large bowl with the lemon grass, kaffir lime leaves, ginger, chilli and garlic, which need to be so finely chopped as to almost make a paste. Add the beaten egg and sesame seeds. Mix well, using your hands.

Heat a griddle pan (or ordinary frying pan). Divide the mixture into 16 and shape into small patties. Cook for 8 minutes on each side.

Serve the chicken cakes with sweet chilli dipping sauce and a salad of rice noodles, chopped peanuts, sliced onion, beansprouts and chopped coriander, if liked.

For Chinese leaf & beansprout salad, as an alternative salad accompaniment, mix 4 tablespoons sunflower oil, 2 tablespoons rice vinegar, 2 tablespoons light soy sauce and 2 teaspoons fish sauce in a bowl. Add 400 g (13 oz) sliced Chinese leaves, 100 g (3½ oz) rinsed and drained beansprouts, 4 sliced spring onions, 250 g (8 oz) carrots cut into matchstick strips, 50 g (2 oz) roughly chopped salted peanuts and 2 tablespoons chopped mint then toss together.
Calories per serving 247

peppered chicken skewers

Calories per serving **216**
Serves **4**
Preparation time **10 minutes,**
  plus marinating
Cooking time **10 minutes**

4 boneless, skinless **chicken
  breasts**, about 150 g (5 oz)
  each
2 tablespoons finely chopped
  rosemary, plus extra to
  garnish
2 **garlic cloves**, finely chopped
3 tablespoons **lemon juice**
2 teaspoons **mustard**
1 tablespoon **clear honey**
2 teaspoons freshly **ground
  black pepper**
1 tablespoon **olive oil**
pinch of **salt**
lemon wedges, to serve

Lay a chicken breast between 2 sheets of clingfilm
and flatten slightly with a rolling pin or meat mallet.
Repeat with the remaining chicken breasts, then cut the
chicken into thick strips.

Put the chicken strips in a non-metallic bowl and add
the remaining ingredients. Mix well, then cover and
leave to marinate in the refrigerator for 5–10 minutes.

Thread the chicken strips on to 8 skewers and cook
under a preheated medium-hot grill for 4–5 minutes
on each side or until the chicken is cooked through.
Garnish with rosemary, and serve immediately with
lemon wedges.

For chicken & sweet chilli sesame skewers, cut
450 g (1 lb) chicken breasts into cubes, put in a small
bowl, drizzle with 2 teaspoons olive oil and season with
salt and pepper. Thread on to skewers and cook under
a preheated hot grill, turning occasionally until cooked
through. Remove from the heat and coat the skewers
with 2 tablespoons sweet chilli sauce and sprinkle with
1 tablespoon sesame seeds. Cook under the grill for a
further minute on each side or until glazed. Serve with a
green salad. **Calories per serving 197**

greek chicken avgolomeno

Calories per serving **218**
Serves **6**
Preparation time **10 minutes**
Cooking time **15–20 minutes**

2 litres (3½ pints) **chicken
  stock**
125 g (4 oz) **orzo, macaroni**
  or other **small pasta shapes**
25 g (1 oz) **butter**
25 g (1 oz) **plain flour**
4 **egg yolks**
grated rind and juice of
  1 **lemon**
salt and **pepper**

To garnish
125 g (4 oz) cooked **chicken**,
  torn into fine shreds
extra **lemon rind**
oregano leaves
lemon wedges

Bring the stock to the boil, add the pasta and simmer for 8–10 minutes until just tender. Meanwhile heat the butter in a separate smaller pan, stir in the flour then gradually mix in 2 ladlefuls of the stock from the large pan. Bring to the boil, stirring. Take off the heat.

Mix the egg yolks in a medium-sized bowl with the lemon rind and some salt and pepper. Gradually mix in the lemon juice until smooth. Slowly mix in the hot sauce from the small pan, stirring continuously.

Stir a couple more hot ladlefuls of stock into the lemon mixture once the pasta is cooked, then pour this into the large pasta pan. (Dont be tempted to add the eggs and lemon straight into the pasta pan or it may curdle.) Mix well, then ladle into shallow soup bowls and top with shredded chicken taken off the carcass, some extra lemon rind and some torn oregano leaves. Serve with lemon wedges.

For green bean & asparagus salad, as an accompaniment, put 250 g (8 oz) trimmed fine green beans in the top of a steamer, cover and cook for 3 minutes. Add 400 g (13 oz) trimmed fresh asparagus and cook for 5 minutes until the vegetables are just tender. Mix together 5 tablespoons olive oil and 3 teaspoons each tapenade and balsamic vinegar and season. Drizzle over 100 g (3½ oz) rocket leaves to serve. **Calories per serving 141**

ginger & honey chicken

Calories per serving **218**
  (excluding noodles)
Serves **4**
Preparation time **15 minutes,**
  plus soaking
Cooking time **10–15 minutes**

1 tablespoon **vegetable oil**
3 boneless, skinless **chicken**
  breasts, chopped
3 **chicken livers**, chopped
1 **onion**, finely sliced
3 **garlic cloves**, crushed
2 tablespoons **dried black**
  fungus (cloud's ears),
  soaked in hot water for
  20 minutes, then drained
2 tablespoons **light soy sauce**
1 tablespoon **honey**
50 g (2 oz) finely chopped
  fresh root ginger
5 **spring onions**, chopped
1 **red chilli**, deseeded and
  finely sliced into strips, to
  garnish
rice noodles, to serve
  (optional)

Heat the oil in a wok over a medium heat and add the chicken breasts and livers. Fry the chicken mixture for 5 minutes, then remove it using a slotted spoon and set aside.

Add the onion to the wok and fry it over a low heat until soft. Remove half the onions from the wok and set aside. Add the garlic and the drained mushrooms and stir-fry for 1 minute. Return the chicken mixture to the wok.

Stir together the soy sauce and honey in a bowl until blended, then pour this over the chicken and stir well. Add the ginger and stir-fry for 2–3 minutes. Finally, add the spring onions and garnish with the reserved onions and strips of red chilli. Serve immediately with medium rice noodles, if liked.

For ginger and honey chicken with pak choi, cook as in the main recipe, adding 1 head shredded pak choi or ½ head shredded Chinese leaves to the wok with the ginger and serve without noodles. **Calories per serving 196**

low-fat lemon chicken

Calories per serving **219**
  (excluding rice)
Serves **4**
Preparation time **12 minutes,**
  plus marinating
Cooking time **8 minutes**

1 **egg**, lightly beaten
2 **garlic cloves**, sliced
2 small pieces of **lemon** rind,
  plus juice of 1 lemon
500 g (1 lb) boneless, skinless
  chicken breasts, cut into
  5 mm (¼ inch) slices
2 tablespoons **cornflour**
1 tablespoon **rapeseed** or
  olive oil
1 **spring onion**, diagonally
  sliced into 1.5 cm (¾ inch)
  lengths
lemon slices, to garnish
boiled rice, to serve (optional)

Mix the egg, garlic and lemon rind together in a shallow dish, add the chicken and leave to marinate for 10–15 minutes.

Remove the lemon rind and add the cornflour to the marinated chicken. Mix thoroughly to distribute the cornflour evenly among the chicken slices.

Heat the oil in a wok over a high heat until the oil starts to shimmer. Add the chicken slices, making sure you leave a little space between them, and fry for 2 minutes on each side.

Reduce the heat to medium and stir-fry for 1 more minute or until the chicken is browned and cooked. Turn up the heat and pour in the lemon juice. Add the spring onion, garnish with lemon slices and serve immediately with rice, if liked.

For warm lemon chicken & herb salad, cook the chicken as above, then toss into a bowl with ½ sliced cucumber, a handful of coriander, 6 torn basil leaves and 50 g (2 oz) wild rocket. Dress the salad lightly with ½ teaspoon sesame oil and 1 teaspoon rapeseed or olive oil. **Calories per serving 242**

spiced chicken & mango salad

Calories per serving **222**
Serves **4**
Preparation time **15 minutes**
Cooking time **5–6 minutes**

4 small boneless, skinless
   chicken breasts
6 teaspoons **mild curry paste**
juice of 1 **lemon**
150 g (5 oz) **low-fat natural
   yogurt**
1 **mango**
50 g (2 oz) **watercress**
½ **cucumber**, diced
½ **red onion**, chopped
½ **iceberg lettuce**

Cut the chicken breasts into long, thin slices. Put 4 teaspoons of the curry paste in a plastic bag with the lemon juice and mix together by squeezing the bag. Add the chicken and toss together.

Half-fill the base of a steamer with water and bring to the boil. Place the chicken in the top of the steamer in a single layer, cover and steam for 5–6 minutes until thoroughly cooked. Test the chicken to make sure it is cooked.

Meanwhile, mix the remaining curry paste in a bowl with the yogurt.

Cut a thick slice off either side of the mango to reveal the large, flat stone. Trim the flesh away from the stone, then remove the peel and cut the flesh into bite-sized chunks.

Rinse the watercress with cold water and tear it into bite-sized pieces. Add to the yogurt dressing with the cucumber, red onion and mango and toss together gently.

Tear the lettuce into pieces, divide it among 4 plates, spoon the mango mixture on top and complete with the warm chicken strips.

For coronation chicken, mix the curry paste and yogurt with 4 tablespoons reduced-fat mayonnaise. Stir in 500 g (1 lb) cold cooked diced chicken and 40 g (1½ oz) sultanas. Sprinkle with 25 g (1 oz) toasted flaked almonds and serve on a bed of mixed salad and herb leaves. **Calories per serving 338**

caribbean chicken skewers & salsa

Calories per serving **236**
  (excluding rice)
Serves **4**
Preparation time **30 minutes,**
  plus marinating
Cooking time **10–12 minutes**

4 tablespoons **pineapple**
  juice (from can below)
1 tablespoon **tomato ketchup**
1 teaspoon **paprika**
½ teaspoon **ground cinnamon**
large pinch **ground allspice**
4 boneless, skinless **chicken**
  breasts, cubed
1 **red pepper**, cored,
  deseeded, cut into chunks
1 **orange pepper**, cored,
  deseeded, cut into chunks
boiled rice, to serve (optional)

For the salsa
220 g (7½ oz) can **pineapple**
  rings in natural juice, drained
2 **tomatoes**, diced
100 g (3½ oz) frozen
  sweetcorn, just thawed
½ **red chilli**, deseeded, finely
  chopped (optional)
1.5 cm (¾ inch) piece **root**
  ginger, finely chopped
fresh coriander, roughly chopped

Put the pineapple juice into a bowl. Stir the ketchup and spices into the juice, add the chicken and toss together. Leave to marinate for at least 30 minutes.

Meanwhile, to make the salsa, finely chop the pineapple rings and put in a bowl with the tomatoes and sweetcorn. Add the chilli (if using), ginger and half the coriander and toss together.

Thread the chicken pieces, then the pepper chunks, on to 12 wooden or metal skewers. Sprinkle the skewers with the remaining chopped coriander. Grill the skewers under a preheated hot grill for 10–12 minutes, turning several times until well browned and the chicken is cooked through.

Serve the skewers with spoonfuls of the salsa and rice, if liked.

For Caribbean rice salad, put 200 g (7 oz) easy-cook brown rice in a saucepan of boiling water and cook for 25–30 minutes or until tender. Drain the rice, rinse well with cold water then drain again. Mix it with the salsa, 150–175 g (5–7 oz) diced cooked chicken, 4 tablespoons toasted desiccated coconut and 1 deseeded and diced red pepper. **Calories per serving 400**

chicken & asparagus salad

Calories per serving **244**
Serves **2**
Preparation time **10 minutes**
Cooking time **5 minutes**

150 g (5 oz) **asparagus**, cut
  into 5 cm (2 inch) lengths
200 g (7 oz) **smoked chicken
  breast**
125 g (4 oz) **cherry tomatoes**,
  halved
300 g (10 oz) can **cannellini
  beans**, drained and rinsed
handful of **chives**, chopped

Dressing
2 tablespoons **olive oil**
2 teaspoons **clear honey**
2 teaspoons **balsamic vinegar**
2 teaspoons **wholegrain
  mustard**
1 **garlic clove**, crushed

Cook the asparagus in a large saucepan of lightly salted boiling water for about 4 minutes or until just tender. Drain and plunge into cold water to prevent further cooking. Pat dry with kitchen paper.

Cut the chicken into bite-sized pieces and transfer them to a large salad bowl. Add the tomatoes, beans, asparagus and chopped chives and mix well.

Make the dressing by whisking the oil, honey, vinegar and mustard with the crushed garlic in a small bowl. Pour the dressing over the salad and toss well to coat.

For chicken, asparagus & haloumi salad, prepare 75 g (2½ oz) asparagus as above and set aside. Heat a griddle pan and cook 2 chicken breasts, each about 150 g (5 oz), for 5–6 minutes on each side or until cooked. Set aside, cover with foil and keep warm. Cut 125 g (4 oz) haloumi cheese into 5 mm (¼ inch) slices and fry for 2 minutes on each side until golden and crispy. Mix ½ teaspoon Dijon mustard, 1½ tablespoons lemon juice, 2 tablespoons olive oil and 1 tablespoon roughly chopped tarragon in a small bowl. Slice the chicken and arrange on serving plates with the haloumi and asparagus. Drizzle over the dressing and serve.
Calories per serving 480

chicken, tarragon & orange salad

Calories per serving **246**

Serves **4**

Preparation time **20 minutes**, plus chilling

Cooking time **1¼–1½ hours**, plus reduction and thinning

1.5 kg (3 lb) **whole chicken**

1 medium **onion**, thinly sliced

grated rind and juice of
   1 orange

1 tablespoon chopped **fresh tarragon** (or 1 teaspoon dried)

1 **bay leaf**

1 tablespoon **olive oil**

½–1 tablespoon **white wine vinegar**

salt and **pepper**

To garnish

1 small **orange**, thinly sliced

small bunch **mustard and cress**

tarragon sprigs (optional)

Put the chicken, onion, orange rind and juice, tarragon and bay leaf in a large saucepan. Pour enough water over the top of the chicken to cover it and sprinkle with salt and pepper to taste. Cover, bring to the boil, and simmer for 1–1¼ hours, until the chicken is cooked.

Lift the chicken out of the saucepan and leave to cool. Discard the bay leaf and onion. Measure the stock, then boil until it reduces to 150 ml (½ pint). Set aside to cool, then chill in the refrigerator.

When the chicken is cold, take the meat off the bones, discarding the skin. Cut the meat into bite-sized pieces and place in a bowl.

When the stock has chilled, remove the layer of fat from the top, then reheat gently to thin it. Stir in the oil, add the vinegar, and season to taste. Pour this dressing over the chicken and toss well.

Serve immediately, garnished with orange slices, mustard, cress and tarragon sprigs, if liked, or cover and chill until required. The salad may also be served on a bed of shredded iceberg lettuce.

For chicken, tarragon & orange tagliatelle, add 125 ml (4 fl oz) half-fat crème fraîche to the cooled and reduced stock. Stir in the diced chicken, then reheat. Add 25 g (1 oz) torn watercress and cook for 1 minute until the leaves just wilt. Toss with just-cooked tagliatelle (approximately 150 g/5 oz per person).
Calories per serving 496

asian chicken parcels

Calories per serving **247**
  (excluding jasmine rice)
Serves **4**
Preparation time **5 minutes**
Cooking time **15 minutes**

4 **boneless, skinless chicken
  breasts**, about 200 g (7 oz)
  each
75 ml (3 fl oz) **light soy sauce**
1 tablespoon **clear honey**
2 **garlic cloves**, sliced
2 **red chillies**, deseeded and
  finely chopped
2.5 cm (1 inch) piece of **fresh
  root ginger**, peeled and
  finely shredded
4 **star anise**
3 **baby pak choi**, quartered
jasmine rice, to serve
  (optional)

Score each chicken breast several times with a knife
and put one on each of 4 x 30 cm (12 inch) squares
of foil.

Combine the soy sauce, honey, garlic, chillies, ginger
and star anise in a small bowl, then spoon over
the chicken.

Arrange 3 pak choi quarters on top of the chicken
breasts. Seal the edges of the foil together to form
parcels, transfer to a baking sheet and bake in a
preheated oven, 200°C (400°F), Gas Mark 6, for
15 minutes until the chicken is cooked through.

Leave to rest for 5 minutes, then serve the parcels with
boiled jasmine rice, if liked.

For Mediterranean chicken parcels, score the
chicken breasts as above, put on the foil squares and
season with salt and pepper. Top with 2 teaspoons dried
oregano, 2 chopped tomatoes, 50 g (2 oz) chopped
pitted black olives, 2 tablespoons drained capers in
brine and a good drizzle of extra virgin olive oil. Cook
in the oven as above. **Calories per serving 277**

nasi goring

Calories per serving **255**
Serves **4**
Preparation time **10 minutes**
Cooking time **10 minutes**

2 tablespoons **vegetable oil**
150 g (5 oz) boneless,
   skinless **chicken breast**,
   finely chopped
50 g (2 oz) cooked peeled
   prawns, defrosted if frozen
1 **garlic clove**, crushed
1 **carrot**, grated
¼ **white cabbage**, thinly
   sliced
1 **egg**, beaten
300 g (10 oz) cold cooked
   basmati rice
2 tablespoons **ketchup manis**
   (sweet soy sauce)
½ teaspoon **sesame oil**
1 tablespoon **chilli sauce**
1 **red chilli**, deseeded and cut
   into strips, to garnish

Heat the oil in a wok or large frying pan, add the chicken and stir-fry for 1 minute. Add the prawns, garlic, carrot and cabbage and stir-fry for 3–4 minutes.

Pour in the egg and spread it out using a wooden spoon. Cook until set, then add the rice and break up the egg, stirring it in.

Add the ketchup manis, sesame oil and chilli sauce and heat through. Serve immediately, garnished with the chilli strips.

For vegetarian nasi goring, crush a garlic clove and stir-fry it in 2 tablespoons oil with 1 chopped carrot and ¼ chopped white cabbage. Omit the chicken and prawns but add 1 finely sliced red pepper, 125 g (4 oz) sliced shiitake mushrooms and 2 heads finely shredded pak choi. Stir-fry for a further 2–3 minutes until the vegetables are soft yet still retaining their shape. Add the remaining ingredients and serve in warm serving bowls. **Calories per serving 225**

peppered chicken & aubergines

Calories per serving **256**
  **(excluding salad and
  bread)**
Serves **4**
Preparation time **15 minutes**
Cooking time **15 minutes**

2 tablespoons **sunflower oil**
6 boneless, skinless **chicken
  thighs**, cut into cubes
1 large **aubergine**, diced
1 **red onion**, sliced
2 **garlic cloves**, finely chopped
2 tablespoons **medium hot
  curry paste**
½ teaspoon **black
  peppercorns**, roughly
  crushed
small bunch **fresh coriander**,
  to garnish

To serve (optional)
tomato salad
bread

Heat the oil in a large frying pan, add the chicken
and aubergine and fry, stirring for 5 minutes until the
aubergine is just beginning to soften. Stir in the onion
and garlic and fry for 5 more minutes, stirring until the
onion and chicken is just beginning to brown.

Mix in the curry paste and peppercorns and fry for
5 minutes until the chicken is a rich golden brown and
cooked through when tested (see page 15). Tear the
coriander into pieces and sprinkle over the top. Serve
immediately with bowls of tomato salad and warmed
bread, if liked.

For curried chicken with mixed vegetables, use a
small aubergine rather than a large one, then mix in
1 diced courgette and 1 diced and deseeded green
pepper along with the onion. Finish with 100 g
(3½ oz) spinach and cook for 2 minutes until just
wilted. **Calories per serving 270**

chicken satay

Calories per serving **257**
Serves **6**
Preparation time **10 minutes,**
 plus marinating
Cooking time **10 minutes**

25 g (1 oz) smooth **peanut**
 butter
125 ml (4 fl oz) **soy sauce**
125 ml (4 fl oz) **lime juice**
15 g (½ oz) **curry powder**
2 **garlic cloves**, chopped
1 teaspoon **hot pepper sauce**
6 boneless, skinless **chicken**
 breasts, cubed

To serve (optional)
Lemon wedges

Combine the peanut butter, soy sauce, lime juice, curry powder, garlic and hot pepper sauce in a non-metallic dish. Add the chicken, mix well and chill for 12 hours or until required.

When ready to serve, divide the chicken cubes between 6 metal skewers and cook under a preheated hot grill for 5 minutes on each side until tender and cooked through. Serve immediately with lemon wedges, if liked.

For miso-grilled chicken, mix 2 tablespoons each soy sauce, dry sherry or rice wine, and 2 teaspoons clear honey and miso paste. Add the cubed chicken and marinate as above. Thread on to skewers and cook as above. Serve with rice and a sliced cucumber and red chilli salad. **Calories per serving 224**

crispy spiced chicken wings

Calories per serving **260**

Serves **4 as a starter**

Preparation time **5 minutes**

Cooking time **18 minutes**

125 g (4 oz) **plain flour**

1 tablespoon **hot chilli powder**

½ teaspoon **salt**

12 **chicken wings**

vegetable oil, for deep-frying

1 **red chilli**, sliced into thin rounds

3 **spring onions**, thinly sliced

1 tablespoon finely chopped **fresh root ginger**

lime wedges, to serve

Place the flour, chilli powder and salt in a large bowl and combine thoroughly. Add the chicken wings and toss well to coat in the flour.

Pour enough oil into a wok to deep-fry the chicken, and heat it to 190°C (375°F), or until a cube of bread dropped into the oil turns golden in 20 seconds. Deep-fry 6 chicken wings for 6–7 minutes, turning them in the oil until golden and crisp, then remove using a slotted spoon and drain on kitchen paper. Fry the remaining chicken wings in the same way.

Lower the chilli, spring onions and ginger into the oil, using a slotted spoon, and sizzle until crisp and the chilli is a vibrant red. Drain thoroughly on kitchen paper.

Pile the chicken wings on to a serving plate. Scatter with the crispy chilli, spring onions and ginger and serve with the lime wedges.

For sweet chilli dip, to serve with the chicken wings, cut 3 slices from a cucumber and finely chop. Stir into a bowl with 1 tablespoon chopped coriander, the grated rind of 1 lime and 1 teaspoon Thai fish sauce (nam pla). Stir in 5 tablespoons sweet chilli sauce. **Calories per serving 65**

bhoona chicken curry

Calories per serving **262**
Serves **4**
Preparation time **10 minutes,**
  plus marinating
Cooking time **8–10 minutes**

125 ml (4 fl oz) **fat-free
  natural yogurt**
juice of 2 **limes**
2 **garlic cloves**, finely chopped
1 teaspoon **ground turmeric**
1 tablespoon **mild chilli
  powder**
1 teaspoon **cardamom seeds**,
  crushed
large pinch of **sea salt**
1 tablespoon **ground
  coriander**
1 tablespoon **ground cumin**
4 boneless, skinless **chicken
  breasts**, cut into strips
1 tablespoon **groundnut oil**
1 teaspoon **garam masala**
handful of roughly chopped
  fresh coriander
steamed rice, to serve
  (4 tablespoons per serving)

Place the yogurt, lime juice, garlic, turmeric, chilli powder, cardamom, salt, ground coriander and cumin in a large non-metallic bowl. Mix well and add the chicken. Toss to coat evenly, cover and marinate in the refrigerator for 6–8 hours or overnight.

Heat the oil in a large nonstick frying pan over a medium-high heat, and stir-fry the chicken mixture for 8–10 minutes until tender and cooked through.

Sprinkle over the garam masala and chopped coriander, stir well and serve with steamed rice.

For masala chicken kebabs, prepare the marinade as above and add 4 boneless, skinless chicken breasts, cut into cubes. Marinate in the refrigerator for 6–8 hours or overnight if time permits. When ready to cook, thread the chicken pieces on to 8 metal skewers and cook under a medium-hot grill for 5–6 minutes on each side or until cooked through. Serve with warmed naan bread or rice. **Calories per serving 234**

kung po chicken

Calories per serving **266**
Serves **4**
Preparation time **5 minutes**
Cooking time **10 minutes**

2 tablespoons **groundnut oil**
2–3 **red chillies**, deseeded
  and sliced
2 **garlic cloves**, finely chopped
400 g (13 oz) boneless,
  skinless **chicken breasts**,
  cut into 1 cm (½ inch) cubes
1 teaspoon **chilli bean sauce**
50 g (2 oz) canned sliced
  bamboo shoots, drained
50 g (2 oz) canned **water
  chestnuts**, drained
1 tablespoon **Chinese rice
  wine** or **dry sherry**
100 ml (3½ fl oz) **chicken
  stock** or **water**
1 teaspoon **cornflour** mixed
  to a paste with 1 tablespoon
  water
50 g (2 oz) **roasted unsalted
  peanuts**
2 **spring onions**, cut into 1 cm
  (½ inch) lengths

Heat the oil in a wok over a high heat until the oil starts to shimmer. Add the chillies and garlic and stir-fry for a few seconds.

Add the chicken and chilli bean sauce and stir-fry for a couple of minutes, then add the bamboo shoots, water chestnuts, rice wine and stock and bring to the boil. Slowly add the cornflour paste, stirring until the sauce has thickened and turned transparent.

Stir the peanuts and spring onions into the dish just before serving.

For coconut rice, to serve with Kung Po Chicken, put 200 g (7 oz) washed Thai jasmine or long-grain rice in a saucepan and add 50 ml (2 fl oz) full-fat coconut milk. Pour in water to a level of 2.5 cm (1 inch) above the rice. Bring to the boil, then lower the heat to a slow simmer. Cover with a tightly fitting lid, cook for 10 minutes, then turn off the heat and let the rice steam in the pan for a further 10 minutes before serving. **Calories per serving 204**

chicken livers with green beans

Calories per serving **269**
Serves **4 as a starter**
Preparation time **15 minutes**
Cooking time **8 minutes**

500 g (1 lb) **chicken livers**
5 tablespoons **groundnut oil**
3 **shallots**, very thinly sliced
½ teaspoon finely sliced **fresh root ginger**
2 **garlic cloves**, finely sliced
1 **green chilli**, very thinly sliced
75 g (3 oz) **green beans**, cut into 1 cm (½ inch) slices
½ teaspoon **caster sugar**
1 tablespoon **malt vinegar**
1 tablespoon **Chinese rice wine** or **dry sherry**
2 tablespoons **oyster sauce**
2 handfuls of shredded **iceberg lettuce**
salt and **black pepper**
dried chilli flakes, to serve

Trim away any white membrane of the chicken livers and pat the livers dry with kitchen paper. Lightly season with salt and pepper and set aside.

Heat the oil in a wok over a high heat until the oil starts to shimmer. Tip in the shallots and give them a quick stir, then add the ginger, garlic and chilli. Fry until crisp but not too dark, then remove using a slotted spoon and drain on kitchen paper.

Toss in half the chicken livers and cook over a high heat for 1 minute on each side until just browned. Set aside and fry the remaining livers in the same way, adding some more oil to the wok if needed.

Return all the livers to the wok, then toss in the beans and stir-fry for 1 minute. Stir in the remaining ingredients and continue cooking until the livers are well coated in a rich sauce.

Spoon on to a serving dish with the shredded lettuce and spoon the crispy shallot mixture over the top. Serve with a small bowl of dried chilli flakes on the side.

For warm chicken liver salad, cook the livers as above, then toss into a bowl with 75 g (3 oz) watercress, approximately 10 cucumber slices and 1 tablespoon toasted sesame seeds. Serve as a starter or light lunch. **Calories per serving 290**

aromatic chicken pancakes

Calories per serving **269**
Serves **4**
Preparation time **10 minutes**
Cooking time **7 minutes**

4 boneless, skinless **chicken breasts**, about 150 g (5 oz) each
6 tablespoons **hoisin sauce**

To serve
12 **Chinese pancakes**, warmed
½ **cucumber**, cut into matchsticks
12 **spring onions**, thinly sliced
handful of **fresh coriander**
4 tablespoons **hoisin sauce** mixed with 3 tablespoons **water**

Lay a chicken breast between 2 sheets of clingfilm and flatten with a rolling pin or meat mallet until it is 2.5 cm (1 inch) thick. Repeat with the remaining chicken breasts. Transfer to a baking sheet and brush with some of the hoisin sauce.

Cook the chicken breasts under a preheated hot grill for 4 minutes. Turn them over, brush with the remaining hoisin sauce and cook for a further 3 minutes or until the chicken is cooked through.

Meanwhile, warm the pancakes in a bamboo steamer for 3 minutes or until heated through.

Slice the chicken thinly and arrange it on a serving plate. Serve with the pancakes, accompanied by the cucumber, spring onions, coriander and diluted hoisin sauce in separate bowls, so that everyone can assemble their own pancakes.

For satay chicken pancakes, in a non-metallic dish mix together 6 tablespoons dark soy sauce, 2 tablespoons sesame oil and 1 teaspoon Chinese five-spice powder, add the flattened chicken breasts and coat evenly with the marinade. Cover and leave to marinate in the refrigerator. Put 4 tablespoons peanut butter, 1 tablespoon dark soy sauce, ½ teaspoon cumin powder, ½ teaspoon ground coriander, a pinch of paprika and 8 tablespoons water in a saucepan and mix together over a low heat. Transfer to 4 small bowls. Cook the chicken and pancakes as above and serve with the satay sauce. **Calories per serving 411**

one-pot chicken

Calories per serving **275**
Serves **4**
Preparation time **10 minutes**
Cooking time **45 minutes**

500 g (1 lb) **new potatoes**
4 **chicken breasts**, about 125
  g (4 oz) each
6 tablespoons **mixed herbs**,
  such as **parsley, chives,
  chervil** and **mint**
1 **garlic clove**, crushed
6 tablespoons **half-fat crème
  fraîche**
8 **baby leeks**
2 **chicory** heads, halved
  lengthways
150 ml (¼ pint) **chicken stock**
pepper

Place the potatoes in a saucepan of boiling water and cook for 12–15 minutes until tender. Drain, then cut into bite-sized pieces.

Make a slit lengthways down the side of each chicken breast to form a pocket, ensuring that you do not cut all the way through. Mix together the herbs, garlic and crème fraîche, season well with pepper, then spoon a little into each chicken pocket.

Put the leeks, chicory and potatoes in an ovenproof dish. Pour over the stock, then lay the chicken breasts on top. Spoon over the remaining crème fraîche mixture, then bake in a preheated oven, 200°C (400°F), Gas Mark 6, for 25–30 minutes.

For baked chicken with fennel & potatoes, cut the potatoes in half and place them in a large ovenproof dish with 1 large fennel bulb, cut into quarters. Omit the leeks and chicory. Pour over the stock and bake in a preheated oven at 200°C (400°F), Gas Mark 6, for 20 minutes. Remove from the oven and lay the chicken breasts over the vegetables. Combine 1 tablespoon chopped parsley with 1 tablespoon Dijon mustard and the half-fat crème fraîche, omitting the garlic, and spoon the mixture over the chicken. Bake for a further 25–30 minutes. **Calories per serving 271**

corn & chicken chowder

Calories per serving **284**

Serves **6**

Preparation time **15 minutes**

Cooking time **about 30 minutes**

25 g (1 oz) **butter** or **margarine**

1 large **onion**, chopped

1 small **red pepper**, cored, deseeded and diced

625 g (1¼ lb) **potatoes**, diced

25 g (1 oz) **plain flour**

750 ml (1¼ pints) **chicken stock**

175 g (6 oz) **canned** or **frozen sweetcorn**

250 g (8 oz) **cooked chicken**, chopped

450 ml (¾ pint) **semi-skimmed milk**

3 tablespoons chopped **parsley**

salt and **pepper**

a few sliced **red chillies**, to garnish

Melt the butter or margarine in a large saucepan. Add the onion, red pepper and potatoes and fry over a moderate heat for 5 minutes, stirring from time to time.

Sprinkle in the flour and cook over a gentle heat for 1 minute. Gradually stir in the stock and bring to the boil, stirring. Lower the heat, cover the pan and cook for 10 minutes.

Stir in the sweetcorn, chicken and milk. Season to taste with salt and pepper, cover the pan and simmer gently for a further 10 minutes until the potatoes are just tender. Taste and adjust the seasoning if necessary. Serve the chowder garnished with the sliced chillies and parsley.

For spicy corn chowder, fry the onion, red pepper and potato in the butter as above with 4 finely chopped red chillies. Add the flour then stir in the stock and simmer for 10 minutes. Stir in the sweetcorn and milk, season and simmer as above until the potatoes are just tender. Garnish with coriander sprigs. **Calories per serving 194**

seared chicken sandwich

Calories per serving **293**
Serves **4**
Preparation time **15 minutes**
Cooking time **5–6 minutes**

250 g (8 oz) **mini chicken
    breasts**
8 teaspoons **balsamic vinegar**
8 slices **granary bread**
6 tablespoons **low-fat natural
    yogurt**
½–1 teaspoon **freshly
    grated hot horseradish** or
    horseradish sauce, to taste
100 g (3½ oz) **mixed salad
    leaves with beetroot strips**
pepper

Put the mini chicken breasts into a plastic bag with half the vinegar and toss together until evenly coated.

Heat a nonstick frying pan, lift the chicken out of the plastic bag with a fork and add the pieces to the pan. Fry for 3 minutes, turn and drizzle with the vinegar from the bag and cook for 2–3 more minutes or until browned and cooked through.

Toast the bread lightly on both sides. Slice the chicken into long, thin strips. Mix together the yogurt and horseradish and a little pepper to taste. Add the salad leaves and toss together.

Arrange the yogurt and salad leaves on 4 slices of toast then add some chicken strips, drizzle over the remaining vinegar, if liked, and top with the remaining slices of toast. Cut each sandwich in half and serve immediately.

For tangy chicken, lemon & garlic toasties, toss the chicken fillets with the juice of ½ lemon and 1 tablespoon olive oil then fry as above but without the vinegar. Toast 8 slices wholemeal bread then spread with 4 tablespoons reduced-fat garlic mayonnaise. Divide the chicken between 4 slices of toast then top with the shredded leaves of 2 Little Gem lettuces and a 5 cm (2 inch) piece cucumber, thinly sliced. Cover with the remaining slices of toast then press together and cut into triangles. **Calories per serving 320**

gingered chicken with soft noodles

Calories per serving **297**
Serves **4**
Preparation time **10 minutes**
Cooking time **12–13 minutes**

2 teaspoons **sesame oil**
2 teaspoons **sunflower oil**
2 boneless, skinless **chicken breasts**, diced
2 **garlic cloves**, finely chopped
2.5 cm (1 inch) piece **root ginger**, peeled, finely grated
300 g (10 oz) pack **ready-prepared stir-fry crunchy vegetables**
50 g (2 oz) **ready-salted peanuts**, roughly chopped
400 g (13 oz) pack **chilled fresh egg noodles**
2 tablespoons **sweet chilli dipping sauce**
3 tablespoons **soy sauce**
2 teaspoons **fish sauce** (optional)
small bunch **fresh coriander**, to garnish (optional)

Pour the oils into a wok or large frying pan. When hot, add the chicken and stir-fry for 5 minutes, until lightly browned. Add the garlic and ginger and cook for 1 minute.

Add the mixed vegetables and stir-fry for 3 minutes. Mix in the peanuts and the noodles and stir-fry for 2–3 minutes until hot. Add the chilli sauce, soy sauce and fish sauce, if using, and cook for 1 minute. Spoon into small bowls, and garnish with torn coriander, if liked.

For gingered chicken with beansprout salad, fry the chicken as above, omitting the stir-fried vegetables and noodles, then leave to cool. Mix 125 g (4 oz) rinsed beansprouts with 1 finely shredded Cos lettuce, 1 carrot and 1 courgette, both coarsely grated. Add the chicken, peanuts and sauces and toss together. Garnish with torn coriander. **Calories per serving 233**

under 400 calories

chicken with leek & asparagus

Calories per serving **301**
Serves **4**
Preparation time **10 minutes**
Cooking time **12 minutes**

1 teaspoon **cornflour**
1 teaspoon **dark soy sauce**
2 tablespoons **water**
1 tablespoon **caster sugar**
1 tablespoon **malt vinegar**
3 tablespoons **groundnut oil**
625 g (1 ¼ lb) boneless,
  skinless **chicken breasts**,
  cut into thin strips
1 tablespoon chopped **fresh**
  root ginger
large pinch of **chilli flakes**
1 **leek**, thinly sliced
300 g (10 oz) **asparagus**,
  halved length- and
  widthways
salt and **white pepper**
boiled rice, to serve (optional)

Mix the cornflour and soy sauce to make a smooth paste, then add the water, sugar and malt vinegar. Set aside.

Heat half the oil in a wok over a high heat until the oil starts to shimmer. Add the chicken strips and season with salt and white pepper. Stir-fry for 3–4 minutes until golden, then remove the chicken with a slotted spoon and set aside.

Return the wok to the heat and pour in the remaining oil. Add the ginger, chilli and leek and stir-fry over a medium heat for 3–4 minutes, until the leeks have started to soften. Stir in the asparagus and cook for 1 minute.

Tip the chicken back into the wok and cook for 1 minute. Pour in the cornflour mixture and cook, stirring, until it becomes a thick and velvety sauce. Serve with rice, if liked.

For rice with leeks, ginger and cumin, as an accompaniment, trim 2 large leeks and wash carefully. Drain them and slice into thin rounds. Heat 1 tablespoon olive oil in a large nonstick saucepan. Add 1 teaspoon grated ginger and 1 teaspoon cumin powder. Add the sliced leeks, season and cook for around 10 minutes, stirring regularly. If necessary, add 1 or 2 tablespoons of water to keep the mixture from sticking. Season to taste. Add 400 g (13 oz) cooked rice to the pan and fluff up the grains with a fork. **Calories per serving 176**

warm chicken salad with anchovies

Calories per serving **303**
Serves **4**
Preparation time **20 minutes**
Cooking time **15–17 minutes**

150 g (5 oz) **green beans**,
thickly sliced

1 small **crisp lettuce**, leaves
separated and torn into
pieces

6 **spring onions**, thinly sliced

175 g (6 oz) **cherry tomatoes**,
halved

275 g (9 oz) jar **mixed pepper
antipasto in oil**

2 boneless, skinless **chicken
breasts**, diced

50 g (2 oz) **fresh
breadcrumbs**

4 canned **anchovy fillets**,
drained, chopped

For the dressing
3 tablespoons **olive oil**
2 teaspoons **sun-dried
tomato paste**
4 teaspoons **red wine vinegar**
salt and **pepper**

Blanch the green beans in a saucepan of boiling water for 3–4 minutes until just tender. Drain, rinse with cold water and drain again.

Put the beans, lettuce, onions and tomatoes into a large salad bowl. Lift the peppers out of the jar, reserving the oil, dice if needed and add to the salad.

Pour 2 tablespoons oil from the pepper jar into a frying pan, add the chicken and fry for 8–10 minutes, stirring until golden and cooked through. Spoon over the salad. Heat 1 tablespoon extra oil in the pan, add the breadcrumbs and anchovies, and stir-fry until golden.

Mix the dressing ingredients together, toss over the salad, then sprinkle with the breadcrumbs and anchovies and serve immediately.

For chicken Caesar salad, mix the green beans with the lettuce, 4 hardboiled eggs cut into wedges, spring onions and lettuce as above, plus 4 chopped anchovy fillets. Cut 75 g (3 oz) bread into cubes and fry in 2 tablespoons olive oil and 25 g (1 oz) butter. Set the croutons aside and fry 2 chicken breasts in the same pan, turning until golden and cooked through. Mix 4 tablespoons reduced-fat mayonnaise with 1 finely chopped garlic clove and the juice of 1 lime. Toss with the salad, then sprinkle with croutons and 40 g (1½ oz) grated Parmesan cheese. **Calories per serving 346**

thai chicken curry

Calories per serving **307**
Serves **4**
Preparation time **5 minutes**
Cooking time **15 minutes**

1 tablespoon **sunflower oil**
1 tablespoon **Thai green
curry paste** (see below)
6 **kaffir lime leaves**, torn
2 tablespoons **Thai fish sauce**
1 tablespoon **soft light brown
sugar**
200 ml (7 fl oz) **chicken stock**
400 ml (14 fl oz) can **coconut
milk**
500 g (1 lb) boneless, skinless
chicken thigh fillets, diced
125 g (4 oz) can **bamboo
shoots**, drained
125 g (4 oz) can **baby
sweetcorn**, drained
large handful of **Thai basil
leaves** or **fresh coriander**,
plus extra to garnish
1 tablespoon **lime juice**
1 **red chilli**, deseeded and
sliced, to garnish

Heat the oil in a wok or large frying pan, add the curry
paste and lime leaves and stir-fry over a low heat for
1–2 minutes or until fragrant.

Stir in the fish sauce, sugar, stock and coconut milk
and bring to the boil, then reduce the heat and simmer
gently for 5 minutes.

Add the chicken and cook for 5 minutes. Add the
bamboo shoots and baby sweetcorn and cook for a
further 3 minutes or until the chicken is cooked through.

Stir through the basil or coriander and lime juice, then
serve garnished with the extra leaves and chilli.

For homemade Thai green curry paste, put 15
small green chillies, 4 halved garlic cloves, 2 finely
chopped lemon grass stalks, 2 torn Kaffir lime leaves,
2 chopped shallots, 2.5 cm (1 inch) piece of fresh root
ginger, peeled and finely chopped, 2 teaspoons black
peppercorns, 1 teaspoon pared lime rind, ½ teaspoon
salt and 1 tablespoon groundnut oil in a food processor
or blender and blend to a thick paste. Transfer to a
screw-top jar. This makes about 150 ml (¼ pint) of
paste, which can be stored in the refrigerator for up
to 3 weeks. **Calories per serving (1 tablespoon) 32**

teriyaki chicken with three seeds

Calories per serving **307**
Serves **4**
Preparation time **20 minutes**,
   plus marinating
Cooking time **16–20 minutes**

4 boneless, skinless **chicken
   breasts**, about 125 g (4 oz)
   each
2 tablespoons **sunflower oil**
4 tablespoons **soy sauce**
2 **garlic cloves**, finely chopped
2.5 cm (1 inch) piece **fresh
   root ginger**, finely grated
2 tablespoons **sesame seeds**
2 tablespoons **sunflower
   seeds**
2 tablespoons **pumpkin
   seeds**
juice of 2 **limes**
100 g (3½ oz) **herb salad**
½ small **iceberg lettuce**,
   torn into bite-sized pieces
50 g (2 oz) **alfalfa** or **brocco
   sprouting seeds**

Put the chicken breasts into a shallow china dish.
Spoon three-quarters of the oil over the chicken, then
add half the soy sauce, the garlic and the ginger.

Turn the chicken to coat in the mixture, then leave to
marinate for 30 minutes.

Heat a nonstick frying pan, then lift the chicken out of
the marinade and add to the pan. Fry for 8–10 minutes
each side until dark brown and cooked all the way
through. Lift out and set aside.

Heat the remaining oil in the pan, add the seeds and fry
for 2–3 minutes until lightly toasted. Add the remaining
marinade and remaining soy sauce, bring to the boil,
then take off the heat and mix in the lime juice.

Mix the herb salad, lettuce and sprouting seeds
together, then spoon over 4 serving plates. Thinly slice
the chicken and arrange on top, then spoon the seed
and lime dressing over the top. Serve at once.

For teriyaki chicken with oriental salad, marinate
the chicken as above and make a salad with 200 g
(7 oz) carrots, cut into thin strips, 4 spring onions, cut
into thin strips, 6 thinly sliced radishes and ½ small
head of Chinese leaves, thinly shredded. Fry the chicken
as above, omit the seeds and then continue with the
dressing as above. Slice the chicken, arrange on the
salad and drizzle with the warm dressing. **Calories per
serving 289**

chicken fillets with soy glaze

Calories per serving **363**

Serves **4**

Preparation time **10 minutes,**
plus chilling

Cooking time **30 minutes**

4 **chicken breasts**

4 tablespoons **dark soy sauce**

3 tablespoons **light**
muscovado sugar

2 **garlic cloves**, crushed

2 tablespoons **white wine**
vinegar

100 ml (3½ fl oz) freshly
squeezed **orange juice**

pepper

To serve

steamed vegetables such as
broccoli

rice (1 tablespoon per serving)

Lay the chicken fillets on a chopping board and slice
each in half horizontally. Place in a large, shallow
ovenproof dish, in which the fillets fit snugly.

Mix together the soy sauce, sugar, garlic, vinegar,
orange juice and pepper and pour the mixture over the
chicken. Cover and chill the dish until you are ready to
cook it.

Uncover the dish and bake the chicken in a preheated
oven, 180°C (350°F), Gas Mark 4, for 30 minutes, until
it is cooked through. Transfer to serving plates and
spoon the cooking juices over the meat.

Serve with steamed broccoli and rice (1 tablespoon
per person).

For chicken breasts with oriental glaze, lay 4
boneless, skinless chicken breasts in a shallow
ovenproof dish. Combine the ingredients for the dressing
as above, omitting the orange juice and adding 2
teaspoons chopped ginger and 2 tablespoons Chinese
cooking wine or dry sherry. Cook in a preheated oven,
200°C (400°F), Gas Mark 6, for 15 minutes, then serve
with a scattering of coriander, steamed vegetables and
rice. **Calories per serving 359**

warm chicken & pine nut salad

Calories per serving **319**
Serves **4**
Preparation time **10 minutes**
Cooking time **15 minutes**

4 tablespoons **pine nuts**
4 boneless, skinless **chicken breasts**, halved horizontally
2–3 teaspoons **paprika**
1 tablespoon **olive oil**
handful of **radicchio leaves**
100 g (3½ oz) **mixed salad leaves**
1 **red onion**, thinly sliced
4 tablespoons **sherry vinegar**
2 teaspoons **Dijon mustard**
2 tablespoons **clear honey**
50 g (2 oz) **raisins**
salt and **pepper**

Heat a nonstick frying pan until hot. Add the pine nuts and dry-fry, stirring continuously, until golden, taking care not to let them burn. Tip them out of the pan on to a plate.

Lightly dust the chicken breast halves with paprika and season with salt and pepper. Heat the oil in the pan and fry the chicken breasts, turning occasionally, for about 10 minutes or until cooked through.

Meanwhile, mix together the radicchio, salad leaves and red onion and place on serving plates. Remove the chicken from the pan and stir the vinegar, mustard and honey into the pan juices. Heat though and add the raisins and pine nuts. Pour the warm dressing over the salad and serve with the chicken.

For chicken, raisin & pine nut pilau, cook 250 g (8 oz) basmati rice in lightly salted boiling water for 10 minutes or according to the instructions on the packet. Cut 4 boneless, skinless chicken breasts into bite-sized pieces and fry in 1 tablespoon olive oil and 1 teaspoon smoked paprika with 1 thinly sliced red onion for 5 minutes. Add the drained rice with 125 g (4 oz) baby spinach leaves, 2 tablespoons raisins and 2 tablespoons pine nuts. Season and stir well to mix.
Calories per serving 463

red chicken & coconut broth

Calories per serving **322**
Serves **4**
Preparation time **10 minutes**
Cooking time **20–21 minutes**

1 tablespoon **sunflower oil**
250 g (8 oz) boned and
    skinned **chicken thighs**,
    diced
4 teaspoons **ready-made red**
    Thai curry paste
1 teaspoon **ready-made**
    galangal paste
3 **dried kaffir lime leaves**
400 ml (13 fl oz) can **coconut**
    milk
2 teaspoons **Thai fish sauce**
1 teaspoon **light muscovado**
    sugar
600 ml (1 pint) **chicken stock**
4 **spring onions**, thinly sliced,
    plus 2 extra to garnish
50 g (2 oz) **mangetout**, sliced
100 g (3½ oz) **bean sprouts**,
    rinsed
small bunch of **fresh**
    coriander

Heat the oil in a saucepan, add the chicken and curry paste and fry for 3–4 minutes until just beginning to colour. Stir in the galangal paste, lime leaves, coconut milk, fish sauce and muscovado sugar, then mix in the stock.

Bring to the boil, cover and simmer for 15 minutes, stirring occasionally until the chicken is cooked.

Create curls by cutting very thin strips from the two spring onions reserved for a garnish. Soak in cold water for 10 minutes, then drain.

Add the remaining spring onions, mangetout and bean sprouts and cook for 2 minutes. Ladle into bowls and tear the coriander over the top. Scatter the spring onion curls over the soup.

For veggie Thai broth, heat the oil, add the curry paste and fry for 1 minute. Add the galangal paste, lime leaves, coconut milk, fish sauce and muscovado sugar. Pour in 200 ml (1 pint) vegetable stock then add 100 g (3½ oz) baby sweetcorn finely sliced with the mangetout. Cover and simmer for 10 minutes. Serve with the coriander as above. **Calories per serving 268**

chicken ratatouille

Calories per serving **333**
Serves **2**
Preparation time **15 minutes**
Cooking time **25 minutes**

2 tablespoons **olive oil**
2 boneless, boneless, skinless
  chicken breasts, cut into
  bite-sized pieces
65 g (2½ oz) **courgettes**,
  thinly sliced
75 g (3 oz) **aubergine**, cubed
150 g (5 oz) **onion**, thinly
  sliced
50 g (2 oz) cored, deseeded
  green pepper, thinly sliced
75 g (3 oz) **mushrooms**,
  sliced
400 g (13 oz) can **plum
  tomatoes**
2 **garlic cloves**, finely chopped
1 teaspoon organic **vegetable
  bouillon powder**
1 teaspoon **dried basil**
1 teaspoon **dried parsley**
½ teaspoon **ground black
  pepper**

Heat the oil in a large frying pan, add the chicken and cook, stirring, for 3–4 minutes until browned all over. Add the courgettes, aubergine, onion, green pepper and mushrooms and cook, stirring occasionally, for 15 minutes or until tender.

Add the tomatoes to the pan and gently stir. Stir in the garlic, bouillon powder, herbs and pepper and simmer, uncovered, for 5 minutes or until the chicken is tender. Serve immediately.

chicken teriyaki

Calories per serving **340**
Serves **4**
Preparation time **5 minutes,**
  plus marinating
Cooking time **5–6 minutes**

4 boneless, boneless, skinless
  chicken breasts, about 500 g
  (1 lb) in total, cut into 2.5 cm
  (1 inch) cubes
4 tablespoons **dark soy
  sauce**, plus extra to serve
4 tablespoons **mirin**
2 tablespoons **caster sugar**
250 g (8 oz) **cooked soba
  noodles**
3 tablespoons **sesame oil**

Place the chicken in a shallow dish. Combine the soy sauce, mirin and sugar, add to the chicken and toss well to coat. Set aside to marinate for 15 minutes.

Meanwhile, cook the noodles according to the packet instructions, then drain, refresh in iced water, drain again and chill.

Thread the chicken cubes on to metal skewers and barbecue or grill for 2–3 minutes on each side.

Toss the noodles with a little sesame oil and serve with the chicken and the remaining sesame oil and soy sauce.

For chicken teriyaki with beans & coriander, cut 4 boneless, skinless chicken breasts into cubes and place in a non-metallic dish. Make the marinade as above and marinate the cubed chicken in the mixture for 15 minutes. Thinly slice and blanch 125 g (4 oz) French beans. Toss the cooked beans with 1 tablespoon sesame oil and a large handful of fresh coriander. Thread the chicken cubes on to skewers and cook under a preheated grill, turning occasionally until cooked through. Serve the skewers with the cooled beans and coriander. **Calories per serving 297**

tandoori chicken skewers

Calories per serving **343**
Serves **4**
Preparation time **10 minutes,**
  plus marinating
Cooking time **about 10**
  minutes

200 ml (7 fl oz) **fat-free**
  natural yogurt
3 tablespoons **tandoori**
  powder
1 tablespoon finely grated
  garlic
1 tablespoon peeled and finely
  grated **fresh root ginger**
juice of **2 limes**
1 kg (2 lb) boneless, skinless
  chicken breasts, cubed
2 **yellow peppers**, cored,
  deseeded and cubed
2 **red peppers**, cored,
  deseeded and cubed
salt and **pepper**

To serve (optional)
naan bread

Place the yogurt, tandoori powder, garlic, ginger and lime juice in a large non-metallic bowl. Mix well, season to taste and add the chicken. Toss to coat evenly, cover and marinate in the refrigerator for 6–8 hours or overnight.

Preheat the grill to medium-hot. Thread the chicken on to 8 metal skewers, alternating with the pepper pieces, and grill for 4–5 minutes on each side until the edges are lightly charred and the chicken is cooked through. Serve with the pomegranate raita (see below) or warmed naan breads, if liked.

For pomegranate raita, to serve as an accompaniment, place 375 ml (13 fl oz) fat-free natural yogurt in a bowl. Coarsely grate ½ cucumber, squeeze out the excess liquid and add to the yogurt with a small handful of finely chopped mint leaves, 2 teaspoons lightly dry-roasted cumin seeds and 100 g (3½ oz) pomegranate seeds. Season, mix well and chill until ready to serve. **Calories per serving 19**

griddled salsa chicken

Calories per serving **343**
Serves **4**
Preparation time **10 minutes**
Cooking time **6 minutes**

4 **boneless chicken breasts**,
  skin on
3 tablespoons **olive oil**
salt and **pepper**

**For the cucumber & tomato
salsa**
1 **red onion**, finely chopped
2 **tomatoes**, deseeded and
  diced
1 **cucumber**, finely diced
1 **red chilli**, finely chopped
small handful of fresh
  coriander, chopped
juice of **1 lime**

Remove the skin from the chicken breasts. Using kitchen scissors, cut each breast in half lengthways but without cutting the whole way through. Open each breast out flat. Brush with the oil and season well with salt and pepper. Heat a griddle pan until very hot. Add the chicken breasts and cook for 3 minutes on each side or until cooked through and grill-marked.

Meanwhile, to make the salsa, mix together the onion, tomatoes, cucumber, red chilli, coriander and lime juice. Season well with salt and pepper.

Serve the chicken hot with the spicy salsa spooned over and around.

For pineapple salsa, as an accompaniment, mix together 6 tablespoons drained and roughly diced canned pineapple, 1 finely chopped red onion, 1 tablespoon finely chopped fresh root ginger, 1 finely chopped red chilli, grated rind and juice of 1 lime, 2 teaspoons clear honey, and salt and pepper to taste. Calories per serving 38

bamboo chicken with cashews

Calories per serving **343**
  (excluding rice)
Serves **4**
Preparation time **10 minutes**
Cooking time **15 minutes**

250 ml (8 fl oz) **chicken stock**
400 g (13 oz) boneless,
  skinless **chicken breasts**,
  cubed
2 tablespoons **yellow bean
  sauce**
200 g (7 oz) **carrots**, sliced
200 g (7 oz) canned sliced
  bamboo shoots, drained
1 teaspoon **cornflour** mixed to
  a paste with 2 tablespoons
  water
125 g (4 oz) **cashew nuts**,
  toasted
1 **spring onion**, shredded
boiled rice, to serve (optional)

Heat the chicken stock in a wok. Add the chicken meat
and bring the stock back to the boil, stirring, then lower
the heat and cook for 5 minutes. Remove the chicken
using a slotted spoon and set aside.

Add the yellow bean sauce to the wok and cook for 2
minutes. Add the carrots and bamboo shoots and cook
for another 2 minutes.

Return the chicken to the pan, bring the sauce back to
the boil and thicken with the cornflour paste. Stir in the
cashews and spring onion just before serving. Serve
with rice, if liked.

For mild chicken curry with peanuts, cook the
chicken as above. Replace the yellow bean sauce
with ½ tablespoon mild Madras paste and cook for 2
minutes, then add the carrot with 200 g (7 oz) broccoli
florets instead of the bamboo shoots. Continue the
recipe as above, finishing by stirring in 125 g (4 oz)
chopped roasted peanuts in place of the cashews and 2
sliced spring onions. **Calories per serving 350**

chicken kofta curry

Calories per serving **343**
Serves **4**
Preparation time **15 minutes**
Cooking time **25 minutes**

750 g (1½ lb) **minced chicken**
2 teaspoons peeled and finely grated **fresh root ginger**
2 **garlic cloves**, crushed
2 teaspoons **fennel seeds**, crushed
1 teaspoon **ground cinnamon**
1 teaspoon **chilli powder**
cooking oil spray
500 ml (17 fl oz) **tomato passata with onions and garlic**
1 teaspoon **ground turmeric**
2 tablespoons **medium curry powder**
1 teaspoon **agave syrup**
salt and **pepper**

To serve
100 ml (3½ fl oz) **fat-free natural yogurt**, whisked
pinch of **chilli powder**
chopped **mint leaves**

Place the mince in a bowl with the ginger, garlic, fennel seeds, cinnamon and chilli powder. Season to taste and mix thoroughly with your hands until well combined. Form the mixture into walnut-sized balls.

Spray a large nonstick frying pan with cooking oil spray and place over a medium heat. Add the chicken balls and stir-fry for 4–5 minutes or until lightly browned. Transfer to a plate and keep warm.

Pour the passata into the frying pan and add the turmeric, curry powder and agave syrup. Bring to the boil, then reduce the heat to a simmer, season to taste and carefully place the chicken balls in the sauce. Cover and cook gently for 15–20 minutes, turning the balls occasionally, until they are cooked through.

Serve immediately, drizzled with the yogurt and sprinkled with chilli powder and mint leaves.

For quick chunky chicken Madras, replace the minced chicken with cubed, boneless, skinless chicken breasts and the medium curry powder with Madras curry powder. Cook as above and add 300 g (10 oz) peas for the last 5 minutes of cooking. Serve hot. **Calories per serving 387**

smoked mustard chicken

Calories per serving **345**
Serves **4**
Preparation time **10 minutes**
Cooking time **20 minutes**

1 tablespoon **wholegrain mustard**
1 tablespoon **extra virgin olive oil**
4 **chicken breasts**, about 175 g (6 oz) each
150 g (5 oz) uncooked **rice**
75 g (3 oz) **Earl Grey tea leaves**
salt and **black pepper**
steamed vegetables, such as broccoli, to serve

For the salsa verde
handful of **flat leaf parsley**
handful of **mint leaves**
handful of **basil leaves**
1 teaspoon **capers**
2 **anchovies** in oil
1 **garlic clove**, crushed
4 tablespoons **olive oil**
1 tablespoon **red wine vinegar**

Stir together the mustard and olive oil and season with salt and pepper. Rub this mixture all over the chicken breasts and set aside.

Prepare a wok for smoking by lining it with foil, then add the rice and tea leaves, mixed together. Place a circular rack in the wok and place the wok over a high heat with the lid on. Heat until smoke starts to escape out of it.

Remove the lid and quickly sit the chicken on the rack. Replace the lid and cook for 3 minutes, then reduce the heat to medium and cook for a further 10 minutes. Turn the heat off and let the chicken sit in the wok for a further 5 minutes while you prepare the salsa verde.

Blend all the salsa verde ingredients in a mini food processor or chop them up finely by hand. Tip into a bowl and adjust the seasoning to taste. Serve the chicken warm or at room temperature with the salsa verde on the side and steamed vegetables such as tenderstem broccoli.

For fennel, lemon & honey smoked chicken, season 2 tablespoons clear honey with salt and pepper and smear all over 4 chicken breasts. Prepare the wok for smoking as above, using the contents of 10 fennel tea bags instead of the Earl Grey and adding the rind of 2 lemons to the mixture. Cook the chicken as above.
Calories per serving 337

chicken & pak choi noodles

Calories per serving **345**

Serves **4**

Preparation time **10 minutes,**
plus marinating

Cooking time **7 minutes**

500 g (1 lb) boneless, skinless
chicken breasts, cut into
thin strips

1 tablespoon **Chinese rice
wine** or **dry sherry**

2 teaspoons **cornflour**

½ teaspoon **sesame oil**

½ teaspoon **salt**

2 tablespoons **groundnut oil**

5 **spring onions,** cut into
5 cm (1 inch) lengths

2.5 cm (1 inch) piece **fresh
root ginger**, cut into
matchsticks

1 **red chilli**, deseeded and
thinly sliced

1 tablespoon **sesame seeds**

3 heads of **pak choi**, cut into
5 cm (2 inch) pieces

2 tablespoons **oyster sauce**

1 tablespoon **water**

300 g (10 oz) **straight to wok
noodles**

Put the chicken in a bowl with the rice wine,
cornflour, sesame oil and salt and leave to marinate
for 30 minutes.

Heat the oil in a wok over a high heat until the oil
starts to shimmer. Tip in the chicken strips, spring
onions, ginger, chilli and sesame seeds and stir-fry for
2 minutes before adding the pak choi. Stir for 1 minute,
then add the oyster sauce and measurement water.
Cook, stirring, for 1 minute, then toss in the noodles
and stir-fry until steaming hot.

For chicken & prawn noodles, follow the recipe as
above, but with 300 g (10½ oz) of chicken and adding
150 g (5 oz) cooked small prawns to the pan with the
pak choi. **Calories per serving 329**

cashew chicken with peppers

Calories per serving **348**
  (excluding rice)
Serves **4**
Preparation time **10 minutes**
Cooking time **15 minutes**

2 tablespoons **groundnut oil**
625 g (1¼ lb) boneless,
  skinless **chicken breasts**,
  cut into 2.5cm (1 inch)
  pieces
50 g (2 oz) **cashew nuts**
2 **red peppers**, cored,
  deseeded and cut into large
  pieces
2 **garlic cloves**, chopped
6 **spring onions**, halved
  widthways and lengthways
salt
boiled rice, to serve (optional)

Sauce
1 tablespoon **Chinese rice**
  wine or **dry sherry**
1 teaspoon **sesame oil**
2 tablespoons **light soy sauce**
½ teaspoon **cornflour**
4 tablespoons **water**

Combine all the ingredients for the sauce and set the mixture aside.

Heat 1 tablespoon of the groundnut oil in a wok over a high heat until the oil starts to shimmer. Season the chicken with salt and tip half of it into the wok. Stir-fry for 2–3 minutes, until golden, then remove the chicken using a slotted spoon and set aside. Heat the remaining oil and stir-fry the rest of the chicken in the same way. Remove and set aside.

Add the cashews and red peppers to the wok and stir-fry for 1 minute. Add the garlic and spring onions and cook, stirring, for a further minute. Return the chicken to the wok and pour in the sauce. Cook for 3–4 minutes until the chicken is cooked through and the pepper is tender. Serve with rice, if liked.

For cashew chicken with peppers & water chestnuts, add 8 halved water chestnuts to the wok with the peppers in the third step. After 1 minute add the garlic and the spring onions, cook for 1 minute, then return the chicken and add the sauce to the pan as described above. Stir in 75 g (3 oz) bean sprouts 1 minute before the end of cooking. **Calories per serving 359**

thai sesame chicken patties

Calories per serving **349**

Serves **4**

Preparation time **15 minutes,**
plus chilling

Cooking time **10 minutes**

4 **spring onions**

15 g (½ oz) **fresh coriander,**
plus extra to garnish

500 g (1 lb) **minced chicken**

3 tablespoons **sesame seeds,**
toasted

1 tablespoon **light soy sauce**

3.5 cm (1½ inch) piece of
fresh root ginger, peeled
and finely grated

1 **egg white**

1 tablespoon **sesame oil**

1 tablespoon **sunflower oil**

**Thai sweet chilli dipping
sauce,** to serve
(approximately 2 tablespoons
per person)

spring onion curls, to garnish
(optional)

Chop the spring onions and coriander finely in a food
processor or with a knife. Put in a bowl and mix with
the chicken, sesame seeds, soy sauce, ginger and egg
white.

Divide the mixture into 20 mounds on a chopping
board, then shape into slightly flattened rounds with
wetted hands. Chill in the refrigerator for 1 hour (or
longer if you have time).

Heat the sesame and sunflower oils in a large frying
pan, add the patties and fry for 10 minutes, turning once
or twice, until golden and cooked through to the centre.

Arrange on a serving plate with a small bowl of
chilli dipping sauce in the centre. Garnish with extra
coriander and spring onion curls, if liked.

For baby leaf stir-fry with chilli, to serve as an
accompaniment, heat 2 teaspoons sesame oil in the
same pan used to cook the patties. Add a 250 g (8 oz)
pack of ready-prepared baby leaf and baby vegetable
stir-fry ingredients and stir-fry for 2–3 minutes until the
vegetables are hot. Mix in 2 tablespoons light soy sauce
and 1 tablespoon Thai sweet chilli dipping sauce. Serve
in a side bowl with the chicken patties. **Calories per
serving 55**

chicken mole

Calories per serving **351**
Serves **4**
Preparation time **25 minutes**
Cooking time **50 minutes**

1 tablespoon **sunflower oil**
500 g (1 lb) **minced chicken**
1 **onion**, roughly chopped
2 **garlic cloves**, finely chopped
1 teaspoon **smoked paprika**
½ teaspoon **dried chilli seeds**
1 teaspoon **cumin seeds**,
   roughly crushed
400 g (13 oz) can **chopped
   tomatoes**
400 g (13 oz) can **red kidney
   beans**
150 ml (¼ pint) **chicken stock**
1 tablespoon **dark brown
   sugar**
50 g (2 oz) **dark chocolate**,
   diced
salt and **pepper**

Heat the oil in a saucepan, add the chicken and onion and fry, breaking up the mince with a wooden spoon until browned. Mix in the garlic, paprika, chilli and cumin seeds and cook for 1 minute.

Stir in the tomatoes, beans, stock and sugar, then mix in the chocolate and seasoning. Cover and simmer gently for 45 minutes, stirring occasionally. Spoon the chilli into bowls to serve.

chicken with orange & mint

Calories per serving **355**
  (excluding couscous)
Serves **4**
Preparation time **5 minutes**
Cooking time **15–20 minutes**

salt and **pepper**
4 boneless, skinless **chicken
  breasts**, about 200 g (7 oz)
  each
3 tablespoons **olive oil**
150 ml (¼ pint) freshly
  squeezed **orange juice**
1 **small orange**, sliced
2 tablespoons chopped **mint**
1 tablespoon **butter**
couscous (approximately 2
  tablespoons per serving), to
  serve (optional)

Season the chicken breasts to taste with salt and pepper. Heat the oil in a large nonstick frying pan, add the chicken breasts and cook over a medium heat, turning once, for 4–5 minutes or until golden all over.

Pour in the orange juice, add the orange slices, and bring to a gentle simmer. Cover tightly, reduce the heat to low and cook gently for 8–10 minutes or until the chicken is cooked through. Add the chopped mint and butter and stir to mix well. Cook over a high heat, stirring, for 2 minutes. Serve with couscous, if liked.

For chicken with rosemary & lemon, bruise 4 sprigs of rosemary in a pestle and mortar, then chop finely. Put the grated rind and juice of 2 lemons, 3 crushed garlic cloves, 4 tablespoons olive oil and the rosemary in a non-metallic dish. Add the chicken breasts and mix to coat thoroughly. Cover and leave to marinate in the refrigerator until required. Cook the chicken breasts in a preheated hot ridged griddle pan for 5 minutes on each side or until cooked through. **Calories per serving 370**

griddled summer chicken salad

Calories per serving **357**
Serves **4**
Preparation time **15 minutes**
Cooking time **45 minutes**

4 x 125 g (4 oz) boneless,
  skinless **chicken breasts**
2 small **red onions**
2 **red peppers**, cored,
  deseeded, cut into flat
  pieces
1 bunch of **asparagus**,
  trimmed
200 g (7 oz) **new potatoes**,
  boiled, cut in half
bunch of **basil**
5 tablespoons **olive oil**
2 tablespoons **balsamic
  vinegar**
salt and **pepper**

Heat a griddle pan (or ordinary frying pan). Place the chicken breasts in the pan and cook for 8–10 minutes on each side. When cooked, remove from the pan and cut roughly into chunks.

Cut the red onions into wedges, keeping the root ends intact to hold each wedge together. Place in the pan and cook for 5 minutes on each side. Remove from the pan and set aside.

Place the flat pieces of red pepper in the pan and cook for 8 minutes on the skin side only, so that the skins are charred and blistered. Remove and set aside, then cook the asparagus in the pan for 6 minutes, turning frequently.

Put the boiled potatoes in a large bowl. Tear the basil, reserving a few leaves intact to garnish, and add to the bowl, together with the chicken and all the vegetables. Add the olive oil, balsamic vinegar and seasoning. Toss the salad and garnish with the reserved basil leaves.

For summer chicken wraps, omit the potatoes and follow the recipe as above. Warm 4 soft tortillas as directed on the pack, then spread with 150 g (5 oz) reduced-fat hummus. Toss the griddled chicken (torn into strips) and the vegetables with 2 tablespoons olive oil, the balsamic vinegar and reserved basil leaves as above. Divide between the tortillas, then roll up tightly and serve cut in half while the chicken is still warm.
Calories per serving 489

grilled gazpacho chicken salad

Calories per serving **359**
Serves **4**
Preparation time **10 minutes**
Cooking time **10–12 minutes**

6 tablespoons **olive oil**
4 tablespoons finely chopped
  basil
3 **chicken breasts**, each about
  150 g (5 oz)
375 g (12 oz) **piquante**
  peppers, (165 g/5½ oz
  drained)
1 bunch of **spring onions**,
  roughly chopped
200 g (7 oz) **cucumber**,
  roughly chopped
250 g (8 oz) **cherry plum**
  tomatoes, halved
4 tablespoons chopped **flat**
  leaf parsley

Put 2 tablespoons of the oil in a shallow bowl with
3 tablespoons of the basil. Brush the mixture over
the chicken breasts. Place the chicken on a foil-lined
grill rack and cook under a preheated hot grill for
5–6 minutes on each side or until golden and
cooked through.

Meanwhile, put the piquante peppers in a large salad
bowl with the spring onions, cucumber, cherry tomatoes
and parsley and toss together. Add the remaining oil
and basil and toss again.

Cut the hot chicken into thin slices and toss into the
salad and serve.

For gazpacho soup with chicken salsa, put 4
quartered tomatoes in a food processor or blender with
3 drained piquante peppers, 4 chopped spring onions,
roughly chopped cucumber and process until thick and
smooth. Add a 400 g (13 oz) can chopped tomatoes
and blend again. Meanwhile, chop 1 cooked chicken
breast, about 125 g (4 oz), into small pieces and mix
with 1 tablespoon chopped parsley. Ladle the cold
soup into 4 serving bowls and top each serving with a
spoonful of chicken salsa. **Calories per serving 100**

spiced roast chicken with lime

Calories per serving **362**
Serves **4**
Preparation time **15 minutes**
Cooking time **25–30 minutes**

8 small **chicken thighs**,
  skinned
1 tablespoon **harissa**
4 tablespoons **clear honey**
2 **limes**, cut into wedges
1 **red pepper**, cored
  deseeded and cut large
  chunks
2 **courgettes**, cut into chunks
1 **onion**, cut into wedges
300 g (10 oz) **new potatoes**,
  halved if large
1 tablespoon **olive oil**
salt and **pepper**

Cut a few slashes across each chicken thigh. Mix together the harissa and honey and rub all over the chicken thighs. Place in a roasting tin large enough to spread everything out in a single layer, with the lime wedges, red pepper, courgettes, onion and potatoes.

Drizzle over the oil, season with salt and pepper and roast in a preheated oven, 220°C (425°F), Gas Mark 7, for 25 minutes, turning occasionally, or until the chicken is cooked and the vegetables are tender. Serve with the juice of the lime wedges squeezed over the chicken.

For pan-fried spicy chicken, cut 8 small boneless, skinless chicken thigh fillets into strips and coat in a mixture of 1 tablespoon harissa and 1 tablespoon clear honey. Heat 1 tablespoon sunflower oil in a large frying pan, add the chicken and fry over a medium heat for 5 minutes. Add 1 deseeded and chopped pepper, 2 chopped courgettes, 1 onion, cut into thin wedges, and 2 limes, cut into wedges. Cook for 10 minutes, stirring occasionally, or until the chicken is cooked and the vegetables are tender. Serve with new potatoes. **Calories per serving 316**

chicken, apricot & almond salad

Calories per serving **366**
Serves **4**
Preparation time **15 minutes**

200 g (7 oz) **celery**
75 g (3 oz) **almonds**
3 tablespoons chopped
   parsley
4 tablespoons **mayonnaise**
3 poached or roasted **chicken
   breasts**, each about 150 g
   (5 oz)
12 **fresh apricots**
salt and **pepper**

Thinly slice the celery sticks diagonally, reserving
the yellow inner leaves. Transfer to a large salad
bowl together with half the leaves. Roughly chop the
almonds and add half to the bowl with the parsley and
mayonnaise. Season to taste with salt and pepper.

Arrange the salad on a serving plate. Shred the chicken
and halve and stone the apricots. Add the chicken and
apricots to the salad and stir lightly to combine.

Garnish with the remaining almonds and celery leaves
and serve.

For grilled chicken with apricot & tomato salad,
marinate 4 chicken breasts, each about 150 g (5 oz),
with 2 crushed garlic cloves, 50 ml (2 fl oz) sweet chilli
sauce and the juice and rind of 1 lime for at least 1 hour.
Remove the chicken from the marinade and transfer
to a heated griddle pan. Cook until golden and cooked
through. Remove the stones and chop 12 apricots into
5 mm (¼ inch) pieces. Mix with 3 ripe tomatoes cut
into 5 mm (¼ inch) pieces and 2 tablespoons chopped
coriander. Whisk together 3 tablespoons red wine
vinegar, 3 tablespoons olive oil, 1 teaspoon brown sugar
and 1 teaspoon soy sauce and pour the dressing over
the salad. Combine well and serve with the chicken.
Calories per serving 331

chicken with spring vegetables

Calories per serving **370**
Serves **4**
Preparation time **10 minutes,**
  plus resting
Cooking time **about 1¼ hours**

1.5 kg (3 lb) **whole chicken**
about 1.5 litres (2½ pints) hot
  chicken stock
2 **shallots**, halved
2 **garlic cloves**
2 **parsley sprigs**
2 **marjoram sprigs**
2 **lemon thyme sprigs**
2 **carrots**, halved
1 **leek**, trimmed and sliced
200 g (7 oz) **Tenderstem
  broccoli**
250 g (8 oz) **asparagus,**
  trimmed
½ **Savoy cabbage**, shredded

Put the chicken in a large saucepan and pour over enough stock to just cover the chicken. Push the shallots, garlic, herbs, carrots and leek into the pan and bring to the boil over a medium-high heat, then reduce the heat and simmer gently for 1 hour or until the chicken is falling away from the bones.

Add the remaining vegetables to the pan and simmer for a further 6–8 minutes or until the vegetables are cooked.

Turn off the heat and leave to rest for 5–10 minutes. Remove the skin from the chicken, if liked, then divide the chicken among 4 deep serving bowls with the vegetables. Serve with spoonfuls of the broth ladled over.

mango & smoked chicken salad

Calories per serving **378**
Serves **4**
Preparation time **15 minutes**

2 ripe **avocados**, halved,
   stoned and peeled
2 tablespoons **lemon juice**
1 small **mango**
handful of **watercress**
50 g (2 oz) cooked **beetroot**,
   finely sliced
175 g (6 oz) **smoked chicken**

Dressing
3 tablespoons **olive oil**
1 teaspoon **wholegrain
   mustard**
1 teaspoon **clear honey**
2 teaspoons **cider vinegar**
salt and **pepper**

Slice or dice the avocado flesh and put it in a shallow bowl with the lemon juice.

Cut the mango in half on either side of the central stone, peel away the skin and slice or dice the flesh.

Make the dressing. Whisk together the oil, mustard, honey and vinegar. Season to taste with salt and pepper. Remove the avocado from the lemon juice and mix the juice into the dressing.

Arrange the watercress and beetroot on 4 plates or in a salad bowl and add the avocado and mango. Drizzle the dressing over the salad and stir to combine. Thinly slice the chicken and top the salad with the meat. Serve immediately.

For smoked chicken, white bean & thyme salad,
rinse and drain 2 x 410 g (13½ oz) cans cannellini beans and mix with 250 g (8 oz) halved cherry tomatoes, 100 g (3½ oz) rocket, 60 g (2¼ oz) pitted green olives and 1 tablespoon chopped thyme. Make the dressing by whisking 1 teaspoon Dijon mustard, 2 tablespoons cider vinegar, 4 tablespoons olive oil and 1 tablespoon chopped thyme. Dress the salad and serve with 175 g (6 oz) thinly sliced smoked chicken.
Calories per serving 347

chicken couscous salad

Calories per serving **378**
Serves **4**
Preparation time **20 minutes,**
  plus marinating
Cooking time **20 minutes**

4 boneless, skinless **chicken
  breasts**, each about 125 g
  (4 oz)
200 g (10 oz) **couscous**
200 ml (½ pint) hot **chicken
  stock**
1 **pomegranate**
rind and juice of 1 **orange**
small bunch of fresh **coriander**
small bunch of **mint**

Marinade
1½ tablespoons **curry paste**
  (tikka masala)
5 tablespoons **natural yogurt**
1 teaspoon **olive oil**
2 tablespoons **lemon juice**

Make a marinade by mixing the curry paste, yogurt and
oil. Put the chicken in a non-metallic dish, cover with half
the marinade and leave for at least 1 hour.

Put the couscous in a bowl, add the hot stock, cover
and leave for 8 minutes.

Meanwhile, cut the pomegranate in half and remove
the seeds. When the couscous is done, add them to the
couscous with the orange rind and juice.

Remove the chicken from the marinade, reserving the
marinade, and transfer to a foil-lined baking sheet. Cook
in a preheated oven, 190°C (375°F), Gas Mark 5, for
6–7 minutes, then transfer to a preheated hot grill and
cook for 2 minutes until caramelized. Cover with foil and
leave to rest for 5 minutes.

Roughly chop the coriander and mint, reserving some
whole coriander for garnish, and add to the couscous.
Thinly slice the chicken. Spoon the couscous on to
plates and add the chicken. Thin the reserved marinade
with the lemon juice and drizzle over the couscous.
Garnish with the reserved coriander and serve
immediately.

For pomegranate vinaigrette, an alternative
dressing for this salad, whisk together 150 ml (¼
pint) pomegranate juice, 2 tablespoons pomegranate
molasses (available from Middle Eastern stores and
some supermarkets), 2 tablespoons red wine vinegar
and 3 tablespoons olive oil. **Calories per serving 468**

sherried chicken stroganoff

Calories per serving **379**
  (excluding rice)
Serves **4**
Preparation time **10 minutes**
Cooking time **about**
  10 minutes

25 g (1 oz) **butter**
2 tablespoons **sunflower oil**
4 boneless, skinless **chicken breasts** about 150 g (5 oz) each, cut into long, thin slices
2 **onions**, thinly sliced
1 teaspoon **paprika**
2 teaspoons **mild mustard**
6 tablespoons **dry** or **medium dry sherry**
6 tablespoons **water**
6 tablespoons **soured cream**
salt and **pepper**

To serve (optional)
boiled rice

Heat the butter and oil in a large frying pan, add the chicken and onions and fry over a medium heat, stirring, for 6–7 minutes or until the chicken and onions are a deep golden colour.

Stir in the paprika, then add the mustard, sherry, measurement water and salt and pepper.

Cook for 2–3 minutes or until the chicken is cooked through, then add the cream and swirl together. Spoon on to plates and serve with rice, if liked.

For chicken & fennel stroganoff, fry the sliced chicken breasts in the butter and oil as above, replacing one of the onions with 1 small, thinly sliced fennel bulb. When golden add the mustard (omit the paprika) and 6 tablespoons Pernod, instead of the sherry, flaming it with a taper. Add the measurement water and salt and pepper as above. Cook for 2–3 minutes or until the chicken is cooked through, then add 6 tablespoons half-fat crème fraîche and stir until just melted. Serve as above. **Calories per serving 427**

indonesian yellow drumstick curry

Calories per serving **383**
Serves **4**
Preparation time **15 minutes**
Cooking time **40–45 minutes**

2 **red chillies**, roughly
   chopped, plus extra to garnish
2 **shallots**, roughly chopped
3 **garlic cloves**, chopped
4 tablespoons chopped **lemon
   grass** (outer leaves removed)
1 tablespoon peeled and finely
   chopped **galangal**
2 teaspoons **ground turmeric**
1 teaspoon **cayenne pepper**
1 teaspoon **ground coriander**
1 teaspoon **ground cumin**
¼ teaspoon **ground cinnamon**
3 tablespoons **Thai fish sauce**
1 tablespoon **palm sugar** or
   brown sugar
4 **kaffir lime leaves**, shredded
400 ml (14 fl oz) **reduced-fat
   coconut milk**
juice of ½ **lime**
8 large **chicken drumsticks**,
   skinned
200 g (7 oz) **baby new
   potatoes**, peeled
10–12 **Thai basil leaves**, to
   garnish

Place the chillies, shallots, garlic, lemon grass, galangal, turmeric, cayenne, coriander, cumin, cinnamon, fish sauce, sugar, lime leaves, coconut milk and lime juice in a food processor, and blend until fairly smooth.

Arrange the chicken drumsticks in a single layer in an ovenproof casserole. Scatter over the potatoes. Pour over the spice paste to coat the chicken and potatoes evenly. Cover and cook in a preheated oven, for 40–45 minutes until the chicken is cooked through and the potatoes are tender. Serve hot, garnished with basil and chopped red chilli.

For tandoori drumstick curry, arrange 8 large, skinned chicken drumsticks in a single layer in an ovenproof casserole. Mix 300 ml (½ pint) fat-free natural yogurt with 4 tablespoons tandoori paste and the juice of 2 lemons. Season and pour this mixture over the chicken to coat evenly. Cover and cook in a preheated oven at 180°C (350°), Gas Mark 4, for 35–40 minutes, then uncover and continue to cook for 10–15 minutes or until cooked through. Serve warm with a crisp green salad. **Calories per serving 360**

barbecued chicken with apple slaw

Calories per serving **384**
Serves **4**
Preparation time **25 minutes**
Cooking time **15 minutes**

6 tablespoons **tomato
  ketchup**
2 tablespoons **Worcestershire
  sauce**
2 tablespoons **red wine
  vinegar**
2 tablespoons **light
  muscovado sugar**
2 teaspoons **English mustard**
12 **chicken wings**

For the apple slaw
1 **dessert apple**, cored, diced
1 tablespoon **lemon juice**
1 **carrot**, coarsely grated
3 **spring onions**, thinly sliced
200 g (7 oz) **white cabbage**,
  finely shredded, core
  discarded
6 tablespoons **reduced-fat
  mayonnaise**
salt and **pepper**

Mix the ketchup, Worcestershire sauce, vinegar, sugar and mustard together. Put the chicken on a foil-lined baking sheet or grill rack, then brush with the ketchup mixture.

Cook the chicken wings under a preheated grill or on a barbecue for about 15 minutes, turning once or twice until a deep brown and the chicken is cooked through.

Meanwhile, mix all the slaw ingredients together in a bowl, then spoon into a bowl. Put the chicken wings on to a plate and serve with plenty of paper napkins for sticky fingers.

For Chinese barbecued chicken wings, mix 4 tablespoons hoisin sauce with 4 tablespoons orange juice, 2 tablespoons Chinese rice wine or dry sherry and 2 tablespoons tomato ketchup. Brush over the chicken and grill or barbecue as above. **Calories per serving 376**

warm chicken ciabatta with salsa

Calories per serving **384**
Serves **4**
Preparation time **15 minutes**
Cooking time **15–20 minutes**

1 tablespoon **olive oil**
2 **chicken breasts**, each
 about 150 g (5 oz), sliced
 lengthways
pepper
1 **ciabatta loaf**, halved
2 **ripe tomatoes**, roughly
 chopped
1 small **red onion**, thinly sliced
3 tablespoons chopped
 parsley
rocket, to serve
reduced-fat mayonnaise, to
 taste
mustard, to taste

Heat the oil in a large, heavy-based frying pan. Toss the chicken breasts with plenty of pepper, add to the pan and cook, turning occasionally, over a high heat for 15 minutes or until golden and cooked through.

Cut the ciabatta loaf halves into 4 pieces and cook them, cut side down, on a preheated hot griddle pan for 1–2 minutes or until lightly toasted.

Mix together the chopped tomatoes, onion and parsley to make a salsa.

Arrange the slices of chicken on the 4 ciabatta bases and top with salsa and rocket leaves. Spread the ciabatta tops with mayonnaise and mustard, place on top and serve.

For hot tomato, caramelized onion & chicken open sandwich, heat 2 tablespoons olive oil and cook 1 finely sliced red onion over a moderate heat, for 15 minutes or until soft and caramelized. Add 1 tablespoon soft brown sugar for the final 1 minute of cooking, then set aside. Make a salsa by mixing 1 finely chopped tomato with 3 tablespoons chopped coriander, season and set aside. Heat 1 tablespoon olive oil and cook 2 thinly sliced chicken breasts for 4–5 minutes or until golden. Slice 1 ciabatta loaf in half and spread with reduced-fat mayonnaise. Top with the hot chicken, onion and salsa. Add rocket leaves and serve. **Calories per serving 444**

chicken with pimento pureé

Calories per serving **385**
Serves **8**
Preparation time **15 minutes,**
 plus cooling
Cooking time **1¾–2¼ hours**

2 kg (4 lb) **whole chicken**
1 **onion**, quartered
1 **carrot**, sliced
2 **celery sticks**, sliced
4 **juniper berries**, crushed
1 **bay leaf**
4–6 stalks **parsley**
6 **peppercorns**, lightly crushed
parsley, chopped, to garnish
courgette slices, griddled, to
 serve (optional)
salt

For the pimento pureé
250 g (8 oz) canned
 pimentos, drained, rinsed,
 chopped
1 tablespoon **tomato purée**
2 tablespoons **mango**
 chutney
200 ml (7 fl oz) **low-fat**
 natural yogurt
salt and **pepper**

Put the chicken, onion, carrot, celery, juniper berries, bay leaf, parsley, peppercorns and salt into a saucepan. Cover with water. Bring to the boil, cover the saucepan and simmer for 1½–2 hours, or until the chicken is cooked when tested. Leave the chicken to cool in the stock. Lift out the chicken, drain and dry it. Reserve the stock, discarding the bay leaf. Skin the chicken and slice the meat from the bones.

To make the pureé, put the pimentos, 2 tablespoons of the reserved chicken stock, tomato purée and chutney into a saucepan and bring to the boil. Transfer to a blender or food processor and blend until smooth. Set aside to cool. Blend the cooled pimento mixture with the yogurt and season to taste.

Arrange the chicken on a serving dish and pour over the sauce. Garnish with the parsley and serve with griddled courgettes, if liked.

For mini chicken meatballs with pimento pureé,

mix 500 g (1 lb) minced chicken with 3 chopped spring onions, 2 cloves of finely chopped garlic, 1 egg yolk and seasoning. Shape into 20 small meatballs, chill for 30 minutes, then fry in 1 tablespoon sunflower oil for 5 minutes. Transfer to a preheated oven 190°C (375°F) Gas Mark 5 for 15 minutes until cooked through. Serve with the sauce as above, rice and a tomato and onion salad. **Calories per serving 366**

jerk chicken wings

Calories per serving **387**
Serves **4**
Preparation time **5 minutes,**
   plus marinating
Cooking time **12 minutes**

12 large **chicken wings**
2 tablespoons **olive oil**
1 tablespoon **jerk seasoning mix**
juice of ½ **lemon**
1 teaspoon **salt**
chopped **parsley**, to garnish
lemon wedges, to serve

Put the chicken wings in a non-metallic dish. Whisk together the oil, jerk seasoning mix, lemon juice and salt in a small bowl, pour over the wings and stir well until evenly coated. Cover and leave to marinate in the refrigerator for at least 30 minutes or overnight.

Arrange the chicken wings on a grill rack and cook under a preheated grill, basting halfway through cooking with any remaining marinade, for 6 minutes on each side or until cooked through, tender and lightly charred at the edges. Increase or reduce the temperature setting of the grill, if necessary, to make sure that the wings cook through.

Sprinkle with the chopped parsley and serve immediately with lemon wedges for squeezing over.

For sweet potato mash, to serve, peel 600g (1 ½ lb) sweet potatoes and cut them into chunks. Steam or boil until tender, then mash with 2 tablespoons crème fraîche and a good grinding of nutmeg. Season with salt and pepper. **Calories per serving 194**

balti chicken

Calories per serving **388**

Serves **4**

Preparation time **15 minutes**

Cooking time **20–25 minutes**

1 tablespoon **groundnut oil**

2 **onions**, thinly sliced

2 **fresh red chillies**, deseeded
   and thinly sliced

6–8 **curry leaves**

200 ml (7 fl oz) **water**

3 **garlic cloves**, crushed

1 teaspoon peeled and finely
   grated **fresh root ginger**

1 tablespoon **ground
   coriander**

2 tablespoons **Madras curry
   powder**

500 g (1 lb) **minced chicken**

400 g (13 oz) **fresh** or **frozen
   peas**

4 tablespoons **lemon juice**

small handful of chopped
   mint leaves

small handful of chopped **fresh
   coriander**

salt

To serve

chapatis (1 per person)

fat-free natural yogurt (2
   tablespoons per serving)

Heat the oil in a large wok or frying pan over a medium heat. Add the onion, chilli and curry leaves, and stir-fry for 4–5 minutes. Add 4 tablespoons of the measured water and continue to stir-fry for a further 2–3 minutes.

Add the garlic, ginger, ground coriander, curry powder and chicken, and stir-fry over a high heat for 10 minutes. Add the remaining measured water and the peas, and continue to cook for 6–8 minutes until the chicken is cooked through.

Remove from the heat and stir in the lemon juice and herbs. Season to taste, and serve immediately with warmed chapatis and yogurt.

For creamy chicken & vegetable curry, heat 1 tablespoon groundnut oil in a large wok or frying pan. Add 1 chopped onion, 1 sliced red chilli, 6 curry leaves, 2 teaspoons each of crushed fresh root ginger and garlic, and 2 tablespoons mild curry powder. Stir-fry for 1–2 minutes, then add 625 g (1¼ lb) diced boneless, skinless chicken breasts. Stir-fry for 3–4 minutes, then add 500 ml (17 fl oz) chicken stock and 200 ml (7 fl oz) reduced-fat coconut milk. Bring to the boil and cook for 12–15 minutes or until the chicken is cooked through. Stir in 200 g (7 oz) frozen peas and cook over a high heat for 4–5 minutes. Season and serve with rice (approximately 3 tablespoons per person). **Calories per serving 470**

lemony poached chicken

Calories per serving **389**
Serves **4**
Preparation time **10 minutes**
Cooking time **1¾–2 hours**

1 **whole chicken**, about 1.5–2
   kg (3–4 lb)
3 **shallots**, halved
2 **garlic cloves**, lightly crushed
1 **celery stick**, roughly
   chopped
1 **rosemary sprig**
8 black **peppercorns**
100 ml (3½ fl oz) **balsamic
   vinegar**
1 **preserved lemon**, chopped
1 small bunch of **sage**, leaves
   removed
2 tablespoons **extra virgin
   rapeseed oil**
salt and **pepper**
steamed vegetables such
   as **asparagus** and **broccoli**,
   to serve

Place the chicken, shallots, garlic, celery, rosemary and
black peppercorns in a large saucepan. Add the balsamic
vinegar and pour in enough cold water to almost cover
the chicken. Place over a medium heat and bring slowly
to the boil, skimming the surface to remove any scummy
froth. Cover and simmer gently for 1 hour.

Add the preserved lemon and half the sage leaves, then
simmer gently for a further 15–30 minutes, until the
juices run clear when the thickest part of the chicken leg
is pierced with a knife. Remove from the pan and place
in a deep dish, cover with foil and leave to rest. Increase
the heat and boil the stock for 20–25 minutes or until
reduced by half. Remove from the heat and leave to cool
slightly. Season to taste.

Heat the oil in a small frying pan and shallow-fry the
remaining sage leaves for 30 seconds until crisp.
Remove with a slotted spoon and drain on kitchen paper.

Cut the chicken meat from the carcass, discarding
the skin, and spoon into shallow bowls with plenty of
cooking broth. Garnish with the crisp sage leaves and
serve with steamed asparagus and broccoli.

For lemony chicken breasts, replace the whole
chicken with 4 large boneless, skinless chicken breasts.
Place in a large saucepan with the garlic, rosemary,
peppercorns, balsamic vinegar and preserved lemon
and just cover with water. Simmer gently for about 12
minutes or until the chicken is cooked through. Cut the
chicken into thick slices and serve in bowls with the
chicken broth, garnished with sage leaves as above.
Calories per serving 276

griddled chicken baguettes

Calories per serving **391**
Serves **4**
Preparation time **10 minutes**
Cooking time **8–10 minutes**

2 small **part-baked granary** or
   seeded baguettes
2 large boneless, skinless
   chicken breasts, about
   300 g (10 oz) in total
1 teaspoon **olive oil**
4 tablespoons **red pepper**
   pesto
2 tablespoons **sunflower**
   seeds
handful of **rocket leaves**
salt and **pepper**

Salad
¼ **cucumber**, halved,
   deseeded and thinly sliced
2 tablespoons chopped **mint**
1 tablespoon **lemon juice**

Place the baguettes on a baking sheet and bake in a preheated oven, 200°C (400°F), Gas Mark 6, for 8–10 minutes, or according to the packet instructions, until crisp.

Meanwhile, lay a chicken breast between 2 sheets of clingfilm and flatten with a rolling pin or meat mallet. Repeat with the remaining chicken breast. Heat a griddle pan over a medium-high heat until hot. Rub the oil over the chicken breasts, season with salt and pepper and cook on the hot griddle for 2–3 minutes or until slightly charred. Turn the chicken breasts over and cook for a further 2–3 minutes or until slightly charred and cooked through but not dry. Remove from the pan, cover with foil and leave to rest.

Make the salad. Mix together the cucumber, mint, lemon juice and a little salt and pepper in a small bowl.

Slice the chicken into thick slices. Cut the baguettes in half lengthways, spread with the red pepper pesto, then fill with the chicken and the cucumber salad. Sprinkle with sunflower seeds and add a few rocket leaves. Cut in half and serve immediately.

For griddled chicken & spicy couscous, prepare and cook 4 chicken breasts as above and cut into thick slices. Meanwhile, cook 300 g (10 oz) wholewheat couscous according to the packet instructions, then fork through 2 tablespoons homemade (see page 192) or shop-bought harissa. Serve the chicken on the couscous with the cucumber salad as above. **Calories per serving 457**

under 500 calories

thai chicken satay

Calories per serving **497**

Serves **4**

Preparation time **30 minutes,**
  plus marinating

Cooking time **16 minutes**

4 boneless, skinless **chicken
  breasts**, cut into thin slices
3 **garlic cloves**, finely chopped
6.5 cm (2½ inch) piece **root
  ginger**, peeled and grated
2 tablespoons **light soy sauce**
2 tablespoons **lemon juice**
1 tablespoon **sunflower oil**
2 **shallots** or ½ **onion**,
finely sliced
1 small hot **Thai chilli**, thinly
  sliced
4 tablespoons **crunchy
  peanut butter**
150 ml (¼ pint) canned **low-
  fat coconut milk**
2 teaspoons **fish sauce**
1 tablespoon **light soy sauce**

To serve
boiled rice (approximately 2
  tablespoons per serving)
green salad (optional)

Mix the chicken with 2 of the garlic cloves, a third of the
ginger, light soy sauce and lemon juice and then leave
to stand for 30 minutes.

Heat the sunflower oil in a small saucepan. Add the
shallots or onion and fry gently until softened but not
brown. Mix in the remaining garlic and ginger and
the chilli, and cook for 1 minute before adding all the
remaining ingredients. Simmer gently for 5 minutes.

Thread the marinaded chicken slices in a zigzag
pattern on to 12 thin metal skewers. Cook under a
hot grill for 10 minutes, turning once or twice until the
chicken is browned and cooked through. Garnish with
lime wedges and serve with rice (about 2 tablespoons
per person).

griddled tandoori chicken

Calories per serving **401**
Serves **4**
Preparation time **10 minutes**,
   plus marinating
Cooking time **16–20 minutes**

4 x 125 g (4 oz) boneless,
   skinless **chicken breasts**
4 tablespoons **tandoori paste**
   or **powder**
4 tablespoons **olive oil**
2 **red onions**, finely sliced
4 **tomatoes**, finely sliced
bunch of **fresh coriander**,
   roughly chopped
4 tablespoons **lemon juice**
lemon wedges, griddled
   (optional), to serve
salt and **pepper**

Using a sharp knife, make a series of small slashes in the flesh of the chicken breasts and rub in the tandoori paste or powder. Leave to marinate in the refrigerator overnight.

Heat 1 tablespoon olive oil in a griddle pan (or an ordinary frying pan). Cook the marinated chicken breasts for 8–10 minutes on each side, allowing the authentic tandoori charred colour to appear, or until cooked throroughly.

Mix the red onions, tomatoes and coriander together with the lemon juice, remaining olive oil and seasoning in a small bowl. Serve the salad with the tandoori chicken, accompanied by lemon wedges, griddled if liked.

For griddled harissa chicken, rub the slashed chicken with 4 teaspoons harissa paste (see page 192) instead of the tandoori paste or powder. Marinate, then fry. Soak 200 g (7 oz) couscous in 450 ml (¾ pint) boiling water for 5 minutes. Stir in 2 tablespoons olive oil, 3 tablespoons fresh chopped coriander and seasoning. Serve with lemon wedges. **Calories per serving 422**

chicken tacos

Calories per serving **403**
Serves **4**
Preparation time **5 minutes**
Cooking time **20 minutes**

1 tablespoon **vegetable oil**
500 g (1 lb) **chicken mince**
2 **garlic cloves**, crushed
30 g (1½ oz) **taco** or **fajita**
  seasoning mix
juice of 1 **lime**
8 **taco shells**

To serve
4 tablespoons **tomato salsa**
  (1 per person)
4 tablespoons **fat-free Greek**
  yogurt (1 tablespoon per
  person)
crisp lettuce, shredded
100 g (4 oz) grated **reduced-**
  fat Cheddar cheese
  (25 g/2 oz per person)
lime wedges

Heat the oil in a frying pan, add the chicken mince and stir-fry, keeping the meat in clumps. Add the garlic and seasoning mix and continue cooking for 15 minutes, adding a little water if the mixture becomes too dry. Stir in the lime juice.

Warm the taco shells according to the instructions on the packet. Spoon in the mince mixture and top with tomato salsa, yogurt, shredded lettuce and grated cheese, with lime wedges on the side.

For Tex–Mex chicken & beans, fry 500 g (1 lb) chicken mince in 1 tablespoon sunflower oil over a high heat with 30 g (1½ oz) taco or fajita seasoning mix for 15 minutes until clumpy and cooked. Add 250 ml (8 fl oz) passata and 220 g (7½ oz) can kidney beans, rinsed and drained. Heat through and serve on thick slices of toast (1 per person) from a crusty loaf. **Calories per serving 328**

thai chicken noodle salad

Calories per serving **404**
Serves **4**
Preparation time **10 minutes**
Cooking time **10 minutes**

250 g (8 oz) **thin rice noodles**
6 tablespoons **Thai sweet
  chilli sauce**
2 tablespoons **Thai fish sauce**
juice of 2 **limes**
2 cooked boneless, skinless
  chicken breasts
1 **cucumber**, cut into ribbons
1 **red chilli**, finely chopped
small handful of **fresh
  coriander**

Put the noodles in a large heatproof bowl and pour boiling water over to cover. Leave for 6–8 minutes until tender, then drain and rinse well under cold running water.

Whisk together the sweet chilli sauce, fish sauce and lime juice in a bowl. Shred the chicken and toss with the dressing to coat.

Add the noodles, cucumber and chilli to the chicken mixture and toss gently to combine. Scatter over the coriander and serve immediately.

For Mediterranean pasta salad, cook 250 g (8 oz) fusilli according to packet instructions and allow to cool. Meanwhile mix together 3 tablespoons each of balsamic vinegar and olive oil and toss with the chicken as above. Add the cooked pasta, and scatter over a small handful of basil leaves instead of coriander. **Calories per serving 399**

thai barbecued chicken

Calories per serving **406**
Serves **4–6**
Preparation time **20–25
minutes,** plus chilling
Cooking time **30–40 minutes
or 10–15 minutes,**
depending on type of
chicken

1.5 kg (3 lb) **whole chicken,**
spatchcocked, or part-boned
chicken breasts
5 cm (2 inch) piece **galangal,**
peeled, finely chopped
4 **garlic cloves,** crushed
1 large **red chilli,** finely
chopped
4 **shallots,** finely chopped
2 tablespoons finely chopped
fresh coriander
150 ml (¼ pint) **thick coconut
milk**
chive flowers, to garnish
salt and **pepper**

To serve
lime wedges

Rub the chicken all over with salt and pepper and place
in a shallow container.

Put the galangal, garlic, red chilli, shallots and coriander
in a food processor and blend to a paste, or use a
pestle and mortar. Add the coconut milk and mix until
well blended. Pour over the chicken, cover and leave to
marinate overnight in the refrigerator.

Remove the chicken from the marinade, place it
on a hot barbecue and cook for 30–40 minutes for
spatchcocked chicken and 10–15 minutes for chicken
breasts, turning and basting regularly with the remaining
marinade. The whole chicken is cooked when a skewer
inserted in one of the legs reveals clear juices.

Leave the chicken to stand for 5 minutes, then chop
it into small pieces with a cleaver. Garnish with chive
flowers and eat with fingers. Serve with the sweet chilli
sauce and lime wedges.

For sweet chilli sauce, to serve as an accompaniment,
wear a pair of plastic gloves and remove the seeds from
15 medium red chillies then finely chop the flesh. Place
the chillies in a saucepan with 250 g (8 oz) granulated
sugar, 150 ml (¼ pint) rice wine vinegar and 150 ml
(¼ pint) water. Heat gently to dissolve the sugar, then
increase the heat and simmer briskly for 20–25 minutes
or until the liquid has reduced to a syrup. Pour the
sauce into a sterilized glass jar or bottle and keep in the
refrigerator until required. **Calories per serving 92**

chicken & aduki bean salad

Calories per serving **408**
Serves **4**
Preparation time **15 minutes**
Cooking time **2–3 minutes**

1 **green pepper**, cored,
   deseeded and chopped
1 **red pepper**, cored,
   deseeded and chopped
1 small **red onion**, finely
   chopped
400 g (13 oz) can **aduki
   beans**, drained
200 g (7 oz) can **sweetcorn**,
   drained
small bunch of **fresh
   coriander**, chopped
50 g (2 oz) unsweetened
   coconut chips or **flakes**
250 g (8 oz) cooked **chicken
   breast**, shredded
small handful of **alfalfa shoots**
   (optional)

Dressing
3 tablespoons **light
   groundnut oil**
2 tablespoons **light soy sauce**
2 teaspoons peeled and
   grated **fresh root ginger**
1 tablespoon **rice vinegar**

Mix together the green and red peppers, onion, aduki beans, sweetcorn and half the coriander in a large bowl. Whisk together the dressing ingredients in a separate bowl, then stir 3 tablespoons into the bean salad. Spoon the salad into serving dishes.

Place the coconut chips or flakes in a nonstick frying pan over a medium heat and dry-fry for 2–3 minutes or until lightly golden brown, stirring continuously.

Scatter the shredded chicken and remaining coriander over the bean salad and sprinkle with the toasted coconut and alfalfa shoots, if using. Serve with the remaining dressing.

For chicken, avocado & coconut salad, dice the flesh of 1 firm, ripe avocado, toss in 1 tablespoon of lime juice and add to the bean salad. Serve as above. **Calories per serving 496**

herby quinoa with lemon

Calories per serving **409**
Serves **4**
Preparation time **15 minutes**
Cooking time **15 minutes**

200 g (7 oz) **quinoa**
1 tablespoon **olive oil**
1 **onion**, chopped
1 **garlic clove**, crushed
4 boneless, skinless **chicken breasts**, sliced
1 teaspoon **ground coriander**
½ teaspoon **ground cumin**
50 g (2 oz) **dried cranberries**
75 g (3 oz) **no-need-to-soak dried apricots**, chopped
4 tablespoons chopped **parsley**
4 tablespoons chopped **mint**
finely grated rind of 1 **lemon**
salt and **pepper**

Cook the quinoa in a pan of lightly salted boiling water for 15 minutes until tender, then drain.

Meanwhile, heat the oil in a large frying pan, add the onion and cook, stirring, for 5 minutes to soften. Add the garlic, chicken, coriander and cumin and cook for a further 8–10 minutes until the chicken is cooked.

Season the quinoa with salt and pepper. Add the chicken mixture, cranberries, apricots, herbs and lemon rind. Stir well and serve warm or cold.

For chicken & apricot moroccan couscous, put 110 g (3½ oz) Moroccan-flavoured couscous in a bowl, cover with boiling water, cover the bowl with clingfilm and leave to stand for 8 minutes. When all the water has been absorbed, stir in 250 g (8 oz) chopped cooked chicken, 125 g (4 oz) no-need-to-soak apricots and a 220 g (7½ oz) can chickpeas, rinsed and drained. **Calories per serving 384**

thai chicken shells with coriander

Calories per serving **410**
Serves **4**
Preparation time **10 minutes**
Cooking time **15 minutes**

1 teaspoon **vegetable oil**
2 **chicken breasts**, about
 150 g (5 oz) each, sliced
1 tablespoon red or green
 Thai curry paste
400 ml (14 fl oz) can **coconut
 milk**
250 g (8 oz) **basmati rice**
3 tablespoons chopped **fresh
 coriander**
3 **spring onions**, sliced
4 **Little Gem lettuces,**
 separated into individual
 leaves
2 **limes**, cut into wedges

Heat the oil in a nonstick frying pan, add the chicken and fry for 2 minutes.

Add the curry paste and continue to fry for 1 minute, then add half the coconut milk, bring to the boil and simmer gently for 10 minutes.

Meanwhile, put the rice in a saucepan with the remaining coconut milk and 100 ml (3½ fl oz) water. Bring to the boil, then reduce the heat, cover and simmer for 10–12 minutes until the liquid is absorbed, adding a little extra water if necessary. Turn the heat off and stir in the coriander.

Put chicken and spring onion slices and some rice on a lettuce leaf and squeeze the lime wedges over the filled shells before eating.

For quick Chinese-style stir-fry, cook 300 g (10 oz) chicken strips for 1 minute in 50 ml (2 fl oz) vegetable oil with 2 teaspoons chopped garlic. Add 150 g (5 oz) sliced green pepper and 5 deseeded and sliced red chillies and cook for a minute, then stir in 75 g (3 oz) sliced onion, 1 tablespoon oyster sauce, 1 teaspoon fish sauce, ½ tablespoon light soy sauce and ¼ teaspoon dark soy sauce. Stir-fry until the chicken is cooked through then serve. **Calories per serving 200**

fast chicken curry

Calories per serving **413**
Serves **4**
Preparation time **5 minutes**
Cooking time **20–25 minutes**

3 tablespoons **olive oil**
1 **onion**, finely chopped
4 tablespoons **medium curry paste**
8 boneless, skinless **chicken thighs**, cut into thin strips
400 g (13 oz) can **chopped tomatoes**
250 g (8 oz) **broccoli**, broken into small florets, stalks peeled and sliced
100 ml (3½ fl oz) **reduced-fat coconut milk**
salt and **pepper**

Heat the oil in a deep nonstick saucepan over a medium heat. Add the onion and cook for 3 minutes until soft and translucent. Add the curry paste and cook, stirring, for 1 minute until fragrant.

Add the chicken, tomatoes, broccoli and coconut milk to the pan. Bring to the boil, then reduce the heat, cover and simmer gently over a low heat for 15–20 minutes until the chicken is cooked through.

Remove from the heat, season well with salt and pepper and serve immediately.

For chicken patties with curry sauce, follow the first stage of the recipe above, then add the tomatoes, 200 g (7 oz) young spinach leaves and the reduced-fat coconut milk (omitting the chicken and broccoli), and cook as directed. Meanwhile, finely chop 450 g (1 lb) cooked chicken breasts. Transfer to a bowl and add 4 finely chopped spring onions, 2 tablespoons chopped fresh coriander, 50 g (2 oz) fresh white breadcrumbs, a squeeze of lemon juice and 1 beaten egg. Season with salt and pepper. Mix well, then form into 16 patties. Roll in 25 g (1 oz) fresh white breadcrumbs to coat. Brush vegetable oil around a large frying pan over a medium heat. Add the patties, cooking in batches, and pan-fry on each side until golden brown and cooked through. Serve hot with the curry sauce. **Calories per serving 490**

burmese chicken noodle curry

Calories per serving **403**
Serves **6**
Preparation time **20 minutes**
Cooking time **about 1 hour**

1 kg (2 lb) boneless, skinless
  chicken thighs, cut into
  bite-sized pieces
2 **onions**, chopped
5 **garlic cloves**, chopped
1 teaspoon finely grated **fresh
  root ginger**
2 tablespoons **sunflower oil**
½ teaspoon **Burmese shrimp
  paste** (belacan)
400 ml (14 fl oz) **coconut milk**
1 tablespoon **medium curry
  powder**
300 g (10½ oz) **dried rice
  vermicelli**
salt and **pepper**

To garnish
chopped **fresh coriander**
finely chopped **red onion**
fried **garlic slivers**
sliced **red chillies**
lime wedges

Season the chicken pieces and set aside. Process the onion, garlic and ginger in a food processor until smooth. If necessary, add a little water to assist in blending the mixture. Heat the oil in a large pan. Add the onion mixture and shrimp paste and cook, stirring, over a high heat for about 5 minutes.

Add the chicken and cook over a medium heat, turning it until it browns.

Pour in the coconut milk and add the curry powder. Bring to the boil, reduce the heat and simmer, covered, for about 30 minutes, stirring from time to time. Uncover the pan and cook for a further 15 minutes or until the chicken is tender and cooked through.

Place the noodles in a bowl, cover with boiling water and set aside for 10 minutes. Drain the noodles and divide them between 4 large warmed serving bowls. Ladle over the curry, and garnish with chopped coriander, chopped red onion, fried garlic slivers, sliced red chillies and lime wedges.

For tofu noodle curry, replace the chicken with 450g (14½ oz) cubed tofu, then add 50 g (1¾ oz) each of baby sweetcorn and mangetout to the curry 5 minutes before the end of cooking. Finish as above. **Calories per serving 313**

yogurt chicken with greek salad

Calories per serving **420**
Serves **4**
Preparation time **10 minutes**
Cooking time **10 minutes**

150 g (5 oz) **fat-free Greek yogurt**
1 **garlic clove**, crushed
2 tablespoons **olive oil**
finely grated rind and juice of 1 **lemon**
1 teaspoon **ground cumin**
4 boneless, skinless **chicken breasts**, cut into bite-sized chunks
200 g (7 oz) **cucumber**, chopped
1 **red onion**, sliced
4 **tomatoes**, cut into slim wedges
16 **black olives**
175 g (6 oz) **feta cheese**, crumbled
1 small **cos (romaine) lettuce**, torn

For the dressing
1 tablespoon **lemon juice**
2 tablespoons **olive oil**
1 tablespoon chopped **fresh oregano** or ½ teaspoon **dried oregano**

Soak 8 small wooden skewers in water and preheat the grill to high. In a bowl, mix together the yogurt, garlic, olive oil, lemon rind and juice and cumin. Add the chicken, stir well and then thread on to 8 skewers. Place on a foil-lined grill pan.

Cook under a preheated hot grill for 10 minutes, turning occasionally, or until the chicken is cooked and beginning to char in places.

Meanwhile, in a salad bowl mix together the cucumber, onion, tomatoes, olives, feta and lettuce.

Make the dressing by whisking together the lemon juice, oil and fresh or dried oregano. Pour the dressing over the salad and lightly mix together. Serve with the chicken skewers.

For yogurt chicken & bulgar wheat salad, prepare the chicken skewers as above. While they are cooking put 75 g (3 oz) bulgar wheat in a pan with 400 ml (14 fl oz) boiling water. Cover and simmer for 15 minutes until the liquid has been absorbed. Cool slightly before mixing with chopped cucumber, 1 sliced red onion, 4 chopped tomatoes, 16 black olives, 175 g (6 oz) crumbled feta cheese and 2 tablespoons each of chopped parsley and chopped mint. **Calories per serving 414**

quinoa salad with seared chicken

Calories per serving **421**
Serves **4**
Preparation time **25 minutes**
Cooking time **22 minutes**

175 g (6 oz) **quinoa**
¼ **cucumber**, finely diced
1 small **green pepper**, cored,
   deseeded, finely diced
6 **spring onions**, trimmed,
   thinly sliced
125 g (4 oz) **frozen peas**, just
   defrosted
grated rind and juice of
   1 **lemon**
1 tablespoon **olive oil**
1 tablespoon **harissa paste**
4 boneless, skinless **chicken
   breasts**, cut into long
   thin slices
small bunch **mint**, finely
   chopped

For the dressing
2 tablespoons **olive oil**
1 tablespoon **harissa paste**
grated rind and juice of
   1 **lemon**
salt

Add the quinoa to a saucepan of boiling water and simmer for about 10 minutes or according to packet instructions until just tender, then drain in a fine sieve.

Make the dressing by mixing the olive oil, harissa, lemon rind and juice and a little salt in a salad bowl. Stir in the hot quinoa and leave to cool, then mix in the cucumber, green pepper, spring onions and frozen peas.

Mix the lemon rind and juice, oil and harissa in a shallow bowl, then add the chicken and toss well. Heat a griddle pan (or ordinary frying pan) and cook the chicken in batches for about 6 minutes, turning until browned on both sides and cooked through.

Stir the mint through the quinoa salad, then top with the warm chicken. Serve warm or cold. Any leftovers can be chilled and packed into lunchboxes the following day.

For hot fruit & nut quinoa with seared chicken,
toss the just-cooked quinoa in the dressing as above. Omit the cucumber, adding 1 deseeded and chopped red pepper instead, and 2 tablespoons sultanas and 50 g (2 oz) diced, ready-to-eat dried apricots in place of the peas. Sprinkle with 40 g (1½ oz) toasted flaked almonds. Top with the chicken and serve hot with extra spoonfuls of harissa. **Calories per serving 499**

noodles & seven-spice chicken

Calories per serving **437**
Serves **4**
Preparation time **15 minutes**
Cooking time **12 minutes**

3 pieces of **stem ginger** from
  a jar, plus 3 tablespoons of
  the syrup
2 tablespoons **rice wine
  vinegar**
3 tablespoons **light soy sauce**
4 skinned and boned **chicken
  breasts**, about 150–175 g
  (5–6 oz) each
1 tablespoon **Thai seven-
  spice seasoning**
3 tablespoons **stir-fry** or **wok
  oil**
3 **shallots**, thinly sliced
125 g (4 oz) **baby corn**,
  halved
300 g (10 oz) **straight-to-wok
  medium** or **thread noodles**
300 g (10 oz) **baby spinach**
200 g (7 oz) **bean sprouts**

Finely shred the pieces of stem ginger. Mix the ginger syrup with the vinegar and soy sauce and reserve.

Halve each chicken breast horizontally and then cut widthways into thin strips. Toss with the seven-spice seasoning.

Heat the oil in a large frying pan or wok and stir-fry the chicken pieces over a gentle heat for 5 minutes until beginning to brown.

Add the shallots and fry for 2 minutes. Stir in the baby corn and fry for 1 minute. Add the noodles and spinach and scatter with the shredded stem ginger. Stir-fry, mixing the ingredients together, until the spinach starts to wilt.

Add the bean sprouts and soy sauce mixture and cook, stirring, for a further 1 minute or until heated through. Serve immediately.

For chicken with pak choi and prawns, prepare the ginger syrup, vinegar and soy sauce as above. Toss 200 g (7 oz) peeled and deveined raw prawns with the chicken in seven-spice seasoning and cook as above. Replace the spinach with 200 g (7 oz) roughly chopped pak choi. **Calories per serving 459**

moroccan chicken & harissa

Calories per serving **438**
  (excluding rice)
Serves **4**
Preparation time **20 minutes**
Cooking time **35 minutes**

1 **onion**, very finely chopped
2 teaspoons **paprika**
1 teaspoon **cumin seeds**
4 x 125 g (4 oz) boneless,
  skinless **chicken breasts**
bunch of **fresh coriander**,
  finely chopped
4 tablespoons **lemon juice**
3 tablespoons **olive oil**
salt and **pepper**
boiled rice, to serve (optional)

For the harissa
4 **red peppers**
4 large **red chillies**
2 **garlic cloves**, crushed
½ teaspoon **coriander seeds**
1 teaspoon **caraway seeds**
5 tablespoons **olive oil**

Make the harissa by heating a griddle pan (or ordinary frying pan). Add the whole red peppers and cook for 15 minutes, turning occasionally. The skins will blacken and start to lift. Place the peppers in a plastic bag, seal the bag and set aside for a while (this encourages them to 'sweat', making it easier to remove their skins). When cool enough to handle, remove the skin, cores and seeds from the peppers and place the flesh in a blender or food processor.

Remove the skin, cores and seeds from the red chillies in the same way. Add the chilli flesh to the blender with the garlic, coriander and caraway seeds and olive oil. Process to a smooth paste. If not required immediately, place the harissa in a sealable container and pour a thin layer of olive oil over the top. Cover and refrigerate.

Clean the pan and reheat it. Place the onion in a bowl, add the paprika and cumin seeds and mix together. Rub the onion and spice mixture into the chicken breasts. Cook the chicken for 10 minutes on each side, turning once. When cooked, remove from the pan.

Place the coriander in a bowl and add the lemon juice, olive oil and a little seasoning. Add the chicken to the bowl and toss well. Serve with the harissa, spinach salad and rice, if liked.

For a spinach salad, as an accompaniment, rinse and tear 400 g (13 oz) spinach and add to a pan with any residual water. Cover and cook for 1–2 minutes until wilted. Stir in 1 clove chopped garlic, 100 g (3½ oz) Greek yogurt, salt and pepper. Warm and serve. **Calories per serving 50**

192

chicken fajitas & no-chilli salsa

Calories per serving **445**
Serves **4**
Preparation time **20 minutes**
Cooking time **about 5 minutes**

½ teaspoon **ground coriander**
½ teaspoon **ground cumin**
½ teaspoon **ground paprika**
1 **garlic clove**, crushed
3 tablespoons chopped **fresh coriander**
375 g (12 oz) boneless, skinless **chicken breasts**
1 tablespoon **olive oil**
4 **soft flour tortillas**

Salsa

3 ripe **tomatoes**, finely chopped
3 tablespoons chopped **fresh coriander**
⅛ **cucumber**, finely chopped
1 tablespoon **olive oil**

Guacamole

1 large **avocado**, chopped
grated rind and juice of ½ **lime**

Place all the ground spices, garlic and coriander in a mixing bowl. Cut the chicken into bite-sized strips and toss in the oil, then add to the spices and toss to coat lightly in the spice mixture.

Make the salsa, mix the tomatoes, coriander and cucumber in a bowl and drizzle over the oil. Transfer to a serving bowl.

Make the guacamole, mash the avocado with the lime rind and juice and sweet chilli sauce, if using, until soft and rough-textured. Transfer to a serving bowl.

Heat a griddle pan or heavy-based frying pan and cook the chicken for 3–4 minutes, turning occasionally, until golden and cooked through. Fill the tortillas with the hot chicken slices, guacamole and salsa, and fold into quarters to serve.

For soured cream chicken tacos, cook the chicken as above and spoon into 8 warmed, ready-made taco shells. Serve 2 per person with ½ tablespoon soured cream and coriander leaves on each. **Calories per serving 339**

greek-style chicken thighs

Calories per serving **450**
Serves **4**
Preparation time **5 minutes**
Cooking time **30 minutes**

2 tablespoons **olive oil**
4 **chicken thighs**
1 large **red onion**, sliced
250 g (8 oz) **cherry tomatoes**, halved
400 g (13 oz) can **chopped tomatoes with garlic and herbs**
4 tablespoons **sun-dried tomato paste**
125 g (4 oz) **kalamata olives**, drained
150 ml (¼ pint) **red wine**
175 g (6 oz) trimmed **green beans**

To serve
50 g (2 oz) crumbled **feta cheese**

Heat the oil in large, heavy-based frying pan and cook the chicken thighs and red onion over a high heat for 5 minutes, turning once, until golden.

Add the cherry tomatoes and stir-fry for 2 minutes, then add the chopped tomatoes and tomato paste and bring to the boil. Reduce the heat, cover and simmer for 15 minutes. Add the olives, wine and the beans and stir again. Re-cover the pan and cook for 5 minutes more until the beans are just tender and the chicken is cooked through.

Serve ladled into warmed bowls and scattered with the crumbled feta.

For Greek salad with mixed herb dressing, chop
½ a cucumber into chunks and put in a salad bowl with 250 g (8 oz) sliced cooked chicken, 250 g (8 oz) halved baby cherry tomatoes and 125 g (4 oz) kalamata olives. Toss together well. Make a dressing by whisking together 4 tablespoons olive oil, 2 tablespoons red wine vinegar, 1 teaspoon Dijon mustard and ½ teaspoon dried mixed herbs. Pour over the salad ingredients and toss well to coat. **Calories per serving 294**

celery, artichoke & chicken salad

Calories per serving **450**
Serves **4–6**
Preparation time **15 minutes**
Cooking time **5 minutes**

6 thin slices of **rye bread**
2 tablespoons **olive oil**
1 leafy **celery head**
100 g (3½ oz) canned or
    bottled **artichoke hearts**,
    drained and grilled
2 tablespoons roughly
    chopped **parsley**
3 **smoked chicken breasts**,
    each about 100 g (3½ oz)
salt and **pepper**

Dressing
1 teaspoon **Dijon mustard**
2 tablespoons **white wine**
    vinegar
4 tablespoons **olive oil**

Arrange the rye bread slices on a baking sheet. Drizzle with olive oil, season with salt and pepper and bake in a preheated oven, 190°C (375°F), Gas Mark 5, for 5 minutes until crispy like croûtons. Remove from the oven and set aside.

Remove the leaves from the celery, reserving all the inside leaves. Finely slice 3 sticks and put them in a large salad bowl with the leaves, add the artichokes and parsley.

Thinly slice the smoked chicken breasts and add to the bowl with the celery and artichokes.

Make the dressing by whisking together the mustard, vinegar and oil. Drizzle over the salad and lightly mix.

Place a piece of rye toast on each serving plate and top with some salad.

For smoked chicken & cannellini bean salad, rinse and drain a 410 g (13½ oz) can of cannellini beans and put them in a large salad bowl. Add 75 g (3 oz) sun-blushed tomatoes (oil drained), 100 g (3½ oz) blanched green beans, 100 g (3½ oz) grilled artichokes and 3 roughly chopped smoked chicken breasts, each about 100 g (3½ oz). In a small bowl whisk 1 tablespoon chopped parsley, 1 tablespoon chopped basil, 1 teaspoon chopped tarragon, 1 crushed garlic clove, 2 tablespoons white wine vinegar and 4 tablespoons olive oil. Season with salt and pepper. Toss the dressing through the salad and serve. **Calories per serving 403**

198

wild rice & griddled chicken salad

Calories per serving **451**
Serves **4**
Preparation time **10 minutes,**
  plus marinating
Cooking time **35 minutes**

1 **garlic clove**, crushed
2 teaspoons **olive oil**
1 teaspoon **balsamic vinegar**
4 small boneless, skinless
  chicken breasts, halved
  horizontally

Rice salad
200 g (7 oz) mixed **wild** and
  basmati rice
2 **red peppers**, roasted,
  cored, deseeded and sliced
3 **spring onions**, sliced
125 g (4 oz) **cherry tomatoes**,
  quartered
75 g (3 oz) **rocket leaves**
75g (3 oz) **soft goats'**
  cheese, crumbled

Dressing
juice of ½ **lemon**
1 teaspoon **Dijon mustard**
1 teaspoon **runny honey**
2 tablespoons **olive oil**

Mix together the garlic, olive oil and vinegar in a non-metallic bowl, add the chicken and coat in the marinade. Cover and leave to marinate in the refrigerator for at least 30 minutes.

Cook the rice in a saucepan of boiling water according to the pack instructions. Drain well and leave to cool, then mix with the peppers, spring onions, tomatoes, rocket and goats' cheese in a large bowl.

Whisk together the dressing ingredients in a bowl and stir into the rice salad. Spoon the salad on to 4 serving plates.

Heat a griddle pan until hot and cook the chicken for 3–4 minutes on each side until cooked through. Immediately before serving, slice the griddled chicken and arrange on top of the salad.

For wild rice, orange & haloumi salad, make the rice salad as above, replacing the red peppers with the sliced flesh of 2 oranges and omitting the goats' cheese. Make the dressing as above and stir into the salad. Cut 200 g (7 oz) haloumi cheese into slices, brush with a little olive oil and season with plenty of black pepper. Heat a griddle pan until hot and cook the haloumi for 1–2 minutes on each side until browned. Arrange on top of the rice salad and serve. **Calories per serving 499**

catalan chicken

Calories per serving **453**
Serves **4**
Preparation time **15 minutes**
Cooking time **25 minutes**

2 tablespoons **olive oil**
40 g (1½ oz) **flaked almonds**
2 **onions**, roughly chopped
8 **chicken thighs**, boned,
  skinned and cubed
2 **garlic cloves**, finely chopped
100 g (3½ oz) **raisins**
200 ml (7 fl oz) **dry sherry**
250 ml (8 fl oz) **chicken stock**
  (see page 14)
small bunch **flat leaf parsley**,
  roughly chopped
salt and **pepper**

Heat a little of the oil in a large frying pan, add the almonds and fry, stirring for a few minutes until golden. Scoop out of the pan and set aside.

Add the remaining oil to the pan, then add the onions, chicken and garlic and fry over a medium heat for 10 minutes, stirring until deep golden. Mix in the raisins, sherry, stock and a little salt and pepper.

Simmer for 10 minutes until the sauce has reduced slightly and the chicken is cooked through. Sprinkle with the parsley and serve.

For Normandy chicken, omit the raisins and add 1 cored and diced Granny Smith dessert apple and 2 teaspoons Dijon mustard, replacing the sherry with 200 ml (7 fl oz) dry cider. Serve topped with spoonfuls of crème fraîche. **Calories per serving 460**

rice noodles with lemon chicken

Calories per serving **458**
Serves **4**
Preparation time **10 minutes**
Cooking time **10 minutes**

4 small boneless **chicken breasts**, skin on
juice of 2 **lemons**
4 tablespoons **sweet chilli sauce**
250 g (8 oz) **dried rice noodles**
small bunch of **flat leaf parsley**, chopped
small bunch of **coriander**, chopped
½ **cucumber**, peeled into ribbons with a vegetable peeler
salt and **pepper**
finely chopped **red chilli**, to garnish

Mix the chicken with half the lemon juice and the sweet chilli sauce in a large bowl and season to taste with salt and pepper.

Lay a chicken breast between 2 sheets of clingfilm and lightly pound with a mallet to flatten. Repeat with the remaining chicken breasts.

Arrange the chicken on a grill rack in a single layer. Cook under a preheated grill for 4–5 minutes on each side or until cooked through. Finish on the skin side so that it is crisp.

Meanwhile, put the noodles in a heatproof bowl, pour over boiling water to cover and leave for 10 minutes until just tender, then drain. Add the remaining lemon juice, herbs and cucumber to the noodles and toss well to mix. Season to taste with salt and pepper.

Top the noodles with the cooked chicken and serve immediately, garnished with the chopped red chilli.

crispy chicken with salsa verde

Calories per serving **458**
Serves **2**
Preparation time **10 minutes,**
  plus marinating
Cooking time **10 minutes**

2 boneless **chicken breasts,**
  skin on
1 teaspoon **olive oil**
1 **garlic clove**, crushed
1 tablespoon **soy sauce**
new potatoes, to serve

Salsa verde
1 handful **fresh mixed herbs**
  (such as **parsley**, **thyme**
  and **basil**)
1 **garlic clove**, roughly
  chopped
2 **cornichons**
1 tablespoon drained **capers**
1 **anchovy**
2 tablespoons **olive oil**
1 teaspoon **white wine**
  vinegar

Make 3 slashes across the skin side of the chicken breasts and transfer to a non-metallic dish.

Mix together the oil, garlic and soy sauce, pour the mixture over the chicken and leave to marinate for 10 minutes.

Meanwhile, make the salsa verde. Mix all the ingredients together in a blender or food processor until they form a chunky paste. Chill until required.

Heat a griddle pan or heavy-based frying pan, add the marinated chicken breasts, skin side down, and fry for 2–3 minutes. Turn and cook for a further 3–4 minutes until they are cooked through.

Serve the chicken with a spoonful of salsa verde and new potatoes (4 per person).

For tomato chicken with Greek salad, prepare the chicken as above, using a marinade of oil, garlic and 1 tablespoon of tomato purée (omit the soy sauce). Meanwhile, make the Greek salad by tossing together 250 g (8 oz) halved cherry tomatoes, ¼ chopped cucumber, 1 small diced red onion and 80 g (3 oz) crumbled feta cheese. Dress with 1 tablespoon of olive oil and 1 tablespoon red wine vinegar and scatter over 1 tablespoon chopped fresh oregano. Season the salad with salt and pepper to taste. Cook the chicken as above and serve with the Greek salad. **Calories per serving 499**

asian steamed chicken salad

Calories per serving **474**
Serves **4**
Preparation time **10 minutes,**
  plus cooling
Cooking time **8–10 minutes**

4 boneless, skinless **chicken
  breasts**, about 150 g (5 oz)
  each
½ small **Chinese cabbage,**
  finely shredded
1 large **carrot**, grated
200 g (7 oz) **bean sprouts**
small bunch of fresh
  coriander, finely chopped
small bunch of **mint**, finely
  chopped
1 **red chilli**, deseeded and
  finely sliced (optional)

Dressing
125 ml (4 fl oz) **sunflower oil**
juice of 2 **limes**
1½ tablespoons **Thai fish
  sauce**
3 tablespoons **light soy sauce**
1 tablespoon finely chopped
  fresh root ginger

Put the chicken breasts in a bamboo or other steamer
set over a large pan of simmering water. Cover and
leave to steam for about 8 minutes or until the chicken
is cooked through. Alternatively, poach the chicken for
8–10 minutes until the meat is cooked and tender.

Meanwhile, make the dressing by mixing together the
ingredients in a bowl.

When the chicken is cool enough to handle, cut or tear
it into strips and mix the pieces with 2 tablespoons of
the dressing. Leave to cool.

Toss all the vegetables and herbs together and arrange
in serving dishes. Scatter over the cold chicken and
serve immediately with the remaining dressing.

For crunchy peanut steamed chicken salad,
finish with 1 tablespoon of crushed unsalted peanuts.
Calories per serving 497

lemon grass chicken

Calories per serving **476**
Serves **4**
Preparation time **15 minutes**
Cooking time **1¾–2¼ hours**

1 tablespoon **sunflower oil**
12 large **chicken drumsticks**
  (remove skin before eating)
1 **onion**, finely chopped
4 **garlic cloves**, crushed
6 tablespoons very finely
  chopped **lemon grass** and
  1 **lemon grass stalk**, halved
  lengthways
1 **red chilli**, finely sliced or
  chopped
2 tablespoons **medium curry
  paste**
1 tablespoon grated **palm
  sugar**
250 ml (8 fl oz) **chicken stock**
salt and **pepper**

Heat the oil in a large, heavy-based casserole dish and brown the drumsticks evenly for 5–6 minutes. Remove with a slotted spoon and set aside.

Add the onion and stir-fry over a low heat for 10 minutes. Add the garlic, chopped lemon grass, chilli and curry paste and stir-fry for 1–2 minutes.

Return the chicken to the dish with the palm sugar and stock. Bring to the boil, season and cover tightly. Cook in a preheated oven at 140°C (275°F), Gas Mark 1 for 1½–2 hours or until tender. Remove from the oven and serve immediately.

For fresh mango salad, as an accompaniment, dice 1 large mango and dress with the rind and juice of 1 lime. Serve cold. **Calories per serving 33**

chicken with burnt chilli paste

Calories per serving **479**
Serves **4**
Preparation time **15 minutes**
Cooking time **15 minutes**

2 tablespoons **groundnut** or
  vegetable oil
3–4 **dried red chillies**, finely
  chopped
2 **garlic cloves**, thinly sliced
375 g (12 oz) boneless, skinless
  chicken breasts, cubed
2 tablespoons **Thai fish sauce**
2 tablespoons **water**
2 teaspoons **sugar**
2 **red chillies**, sliced
10 **Thai basil leaves**, plus
  sprigs to garnish
4 **kaffir lime leaves**, shredded
125 g (4 oz) **roasted cashew
  nuts**

Burnt chilli paste
2 tablespoons **groundnut oil**
1 **red onion**, finely chopped
6–8 large **dried red chillies**,
  finely chopped
6 **garlic cloves**, finely chopped
2 tablespoons **fish sauce**
1 tablespoon **tamarind water**
2 tablespoons **soft brown
  sugar**

Make the burnt chilli paste first. Heat the oil, add the onion and fry until softened. Remove using a slotted spoon and set aside. Add the chillies and fry until blackened, then remove and set aside. Add the garlic and fry until golden brown, then remove.

Grind half the fried chillies coarsely in a pestle and mortar. Add the onion and garlic and blend to a coarse paste. Return the mixture to the oil remaining in the wok and add the fish sauce, tamarind water and sugar. Heat gently for 2–3 minutes, stirring constantly, then remove from the heat.

Heat the oil in a wok over a high heat until the oil starts to shimmer. Fry the dried chillies until blackened, then remove using a slotted spoon and set aside. Add the sliced garlic to the wok and stir-fry until beginning to brown.

Add the chicken and fry quickly on all sides. Crumble the fried chillies over the chicken and add the burnt chilli paste, fish sauce, measurement water, sugar and one of the sliced chillies to the pan. Stir-fry over a high heat.

Add the basil leaves, kaffir lime leaves and cashew nuts and stir-fry for a further 1 minute. Garnish with the remaining sliced red chilli and the basil sprigs.

For chicken, asparagus & burnt chilli paste, cook the chicken and burnt chilli paste as above. Add 200 g (7 oz) asparagus spears cut in half lengthways to the pan and stir-fry for 5 minutes before serving. **Calories per serving 491**

sweet-glazed chicken

Calories per serving **494**
Serves **4**
Preparation time **10 minutes**
Cooking time **45 minutes**

2 tablespoons **olive oil**
4 boneless, skinless **chicken breasts**, about 150 g (5 oz) each
8 **fresh apricots**, halved and stoned
2 **pears**, peeled, quartered and cored
500 g (1 lb) **new potatoes**
1 **onion**, cut into wedges
grated rind and juice of
  2 **oranges**
a few **thyme sprigs**, chopped
1 tablespoon **wholegrain mustard**
1 tablespoon **clear honey**
4 tablespoons **half-fat crème fraîche**
pepper

To serve
green beans (optional)

Heat the oil in a flameproof casserole, season the chicken with salt and pepper and add to the pan. Fry for 2–3 minutes on each side until golden, then add the apricots, pears, potatoes and onion.

Mix together the orange rind and juice, thyme, mustard and honey and pour over the chicken. Cover the dish with foil and bake in a preheated oven, 180°C (350°F), Gas Mark 4, for 40 minutes, removing the foil halfway through the cooking time.

When the chicken is cooked, stir the crème fraîche into the sauce and serve with green beans.

chicken & barley

Calories per serving **486**
Serves **4**
Preparation time **15 minutes**
Cooking time **about 1 hour
10 minutes**

2 tablespoons **olive oil**
6 boneless, skinless **chicken
  thighs**, diced
1 **onion**, roughly chopped
2 **garlic cloves**, finely chopped
200 g (7 oz) **chestnut
  mushrooms**, sliced
250 g (8 oz) **pearl barley**
200 ml (7 fl oz) **red wine**
1.2 litres (2 pints) **chicken
  stock**
salt and **pepper**
parsley leaves, to garnish

To serve
4 teaspoons **Parmesan
  cheese** shavings

Heat the oil in a large frying pan over a medium-high heat, add the chicken and onion and fry for 5 minutes, stirring until lightly browned.

Stir in the garlic and mushrooms and fry for 2 minutes, then mix in the pearl barley. Add the red wine, half the stock and season with plenty of salt and pepper, then bring to the boil, stirring continuously. Reduce the heat, cover and simmer for 1 hour, topping up with extra stock as needed, until the chicken is cooked through and the barley is soft.

Spoon into shallow bowls and garnish with the parsley. Sprinkle over the Parmesan shavings and serve.

For chicken & red barley, fry the chicken and 1 chopped red onion as above. Add the garlic and 200 g (7 oz) skinned and diced tomatoes, omitting the mushrooms and pearl barley. Stir in 250 g (8 oz) red Camargue rice, cook for 1 minute, then add the red wine. Gradually add the hot stock a small ladleful at a time and stirring constantly, only adding more once the rice has absorbed the previous ladleful. Continue until all the liquid has been absorbed and the chicken and rice are tender. This should take about 25 minutes. **Calories per serving 452**

chicken tagine

Calories per serving **486**
Serves **4**
Preparation time **20 minutes**,
   plus marinating
Cooking time
   1 hour 40 minutes

8 large boneless, skinless
   chicken thighs or 1 **whole
   chicken**, jointed
1 teaspoon **ground cumin**
1 teaspoon **ground coriander**
½ teaspoon **ground turmeric**
1 teaspoon **ground ginger**
1 teaspoon **paprika**
3 tablespoons **olive oil**
2 **onions**, cut into wedges
2 **garlic cloves**, finely sliced
1 **fennel bulb**, sliced
300 g (10 oz) small **new
   potatoes**
handful of **sultanas**
8 **ready-to-eat dried apricots**
75 g (3 oz) **green olives in
   brine** (optional)
pinch of **saffron threads**
400 ml (14 fl oz) hot **chicken
   stock** (see page 14)
small bunch of **fresh
   coriander**, chopped
salt and **black pepper**

Slash each piece of chicken 2–3 times with a small knife. Mix together the spices and half the olive oil, rub over the chicken pieces, cover and marinate in the refrigerator for at least 2 hours, preferably overnight.

Heat the remaining oil in a tagine or large flameproof casserole, add the chicken pieces and fry for 4–5 minutes until golden all over. Add the onion, garlic and fennel to the pan and continue to fry for 2–3 minutes.

Add all the remaining ingredients, except the coriander, and stir well. Cover and simmer for about 1½ hours or until the chicken begins to fall off the bone. Season well and stir in the coriander.

For chicken tagine with prunes & almonds, make the recipe as above, but replace the apricots with 6 chopped prunes. Cover and simmer for about 1½ hours or until the chicken begins to fall off the bone. Stir in 20g toasted flaked almonds with the coriander before serving. **Calories per serving 499**

chicken with black bean sauce

Calories per serving **486**
Serves **4**
Preparation time **10 minutes**
Cooking time **20 minutes**

1 **egg white**
1 tablespoon **cornflour**
2 boneless, skinless **chicken breasts**, about 400 g (13 oz) in total, cut into thin strips across the grain
about 300 ml (½ pint) **groundnut oil**
1 **green pepper**, cored, deseeded and cut lengthways into thin strips
1 **green chilli**, deseeded and very finely shredded
4 **garlic cloves**, cut into very thin strips
4 **spring onions**, shredded
4 tablespoons **black bean sauce**
300 ml (½ pint) hot **chicken stock**
salt and **pepper**
1–2 heaped tablespoons canned **fermented black beans**, rinsed, to garnish
egg noodles, to serve

Put the egg white into a bowl with a little salt and pepper and whisk with a fork until frothy. Sift in the cornflour and whisk to mix, then add the chicken and stir until coated.

Heat the oil in a wok until very hot, but not smoking. Add about one-quarter of the chicken strips and stir to separate. Stir-fry for 30–60 seconds, until the chicken turns white on all sides. Lift out with a slotted spoon and drain on kitchen paper. Repeat with the remaining chicken. Very carefully pour off all but about 1 tablespoon of the hot oil from the wok.

Return the wok to a low heat and add the green pepper, chilli, garlic and about half of the spring onions. Stir-fry for a few minutes, until the pepper begins to soften, then add the black bean sauce and stir to mix. Pour in the stock, increase the heat to high and bring to the boil, stirring constantly.

Add the chicken to the sauce and cook over a moderate to high heat, stirring frequently, for 5 minutes. Taste for seasoning. Serve hot with egg noodles, garnished with the remaining spring onions and the black beans.

griddled chicken with coriander aïoli

Calories per serving **487**
Serves **4**
Preparation time **15 minutes**
Cooking time **10 minutes**

2 teaspoons coarsely crushed
   black peppercorns
4 boneless, skinless **chicken
   breasts**, thinly sliced
1 tablespoon **olive oil**

For the coriander aïoli
small bunch of **fresh
   coriander**, leaves only
1 **garlic clove**, peeled
2 teaspoons **Dijon mustard**
1 **egg yolk**
2 teaspoons **white wine
   vinegar**
150 ml (¼ pint) **sunflower oil**
salt and **pepper**

To serve
green salad
grated beetroot

Make the coriander aioli. Reserve a few coriander for garnish and place the rest in a small food processor or blender with the garlic, mustard, egg yolk and vinegar.

Blend until finely chopped. With the motor running, slowly drizzle in the oil until the mixture is smooth and thick. Season with salt and pepper.

Scatter the crushed peppercorns over the chicken slices and drizzle with oil. Cook, in batches, on a preheated hot griddle for 1–2 minutes on each side or until cooked through and golden.

Garnish the warm chicken slices with the reserved coriander and serve with the coriander aïoli, green salad leaves and grated beetroot.

For griddled chicken with garlic mayonnaise, thinly slice 4 boneless, skinless chicken breasts, sprinkle with 2 teaspoons coarsely crushed black peppercorns and drizzle over 1 tablespoon olive oil. Cook, in batches, on a preheated hot griddle for 1–2 minutes each side or until cooked through and golden. Stir 1 crushed garlic clove into 150 ml (¼ pint) ready-made, reduced-fat mayonnaise. Serve with mixed green salad leaves.
Calories per serving 280

pan-fried chicken wraps

Calories per serving **487**
Serves **4**
Preparation time **15 minutes**
Cooking time **5 minutes**

1 tablespoon **olive oil**
3 boneless, skinless **chicken breasts**, about 150 g (5 oz) each, thinly sliced into strips
3 tablespoons **clear honey**
1 teaspoon **wholegrain mustard**
4 **soft flour tortillas**

Coleslaw
¼ small **white cabbage**, finely shredded
1 large **carrot**, grated
3 tablespoons **olive oil**
2 tablespoons **red wine vinegar**
1 teaspoon **Dijon mustard**
2 tablespoons chopped **parsley**

Make the coleslaw. Put the white cabbage in a large mixing bowl with the carrot and toss together well. In a small jug whisk together the oil, vinegar and mustard. Pour over the cabbage and carrot and toss well to coat. Add the parsley and toss again. Set aside.

Heat the oil in a large nonstick frying pan and cook the chicken strips over a high heat for 4–5 minutes until golden and cooked through. Remove from the heat and add the honey and mustard. Toss well to coat.

Warm the tortillas in a microwave for 10 seconds on high (or in a warm oven), then spread each with the coleslaw and top with the chicken pieces. Wrap each tightly, then cut in half to serve.

For maple-glazed chicken wraps, follow the recipe as above and toss the cooked chicken with 2 tablespoons maple syrup (instead of the honey) and the mustard. Assemble the wraps and serve immediately. **Calories per serving 499**

chicken skewers with couscous

Calories per serving **496**
Serves **4**
Preparation time **25 minutes,**
  plus marinating
Cooking time **20–25 minutes**

480 g (1 lb) boneless, skinless
  chicken breasts
2 tablespoons **olive oil**
2 **garlic cloves**, crushed
½ teaspoon each **ground
  cumin, turmeric, paprika**
2 teaspoons **lemon juice**

For the couscous
2 tablespoons **olive oil**
1 small **onion**, finely chopped
1 **garlic clove**, crushed
1 teaspoon each **ground
  cumin, cinnamon, pepper,
  ginger**
50 g (2 oz) **dried apricots**
30 g (1 oz) **blanched
  almonds**, toasted
175 g (6 oz) **couscous**
600 ml (1 pint) **vegetable
  stock**, boiling
1 tablespoon **lemon juice**
2 tablespoons chopped **fresh
  coriander**
salt and **pepper**

Cut the chicken into long thin strips, place them in a shallow dish and add the olive oil, garlic, spices and lemon juice. Stir well, then cover and leave to marinate for 2 hours. Thread the chicken strips on to 8 small, presoaked wooden skewers.

Prepare the couscous by heating half the oil in a saucepan and frying the onion, garlic and spices for 5 minutes. Chop and stir in the dried apricots and almonds and remove from the heat.

Meanwhile, put the couscous in a heatproof bowl, add the boiling stock and cover with a tea towel and steam for 8–10 minutes, until the grains are fluffed up and the liquid absorbed. Stir in the remaining oil and the fruit and nut mixture, add the lemon juice and coriander and season to taste.

While the couscous is steaming, griddle or grill the chicken skewers for 4–5 minutes on each side, until charred and cooked through. Serve with the couscous, garnished with pomegranate seeds, lemon wedges and coriander sprigs, if liked.

For roasted chicken with herb couscous, mix the oil, garlic, spices and lemon juice and drizzle over 4 large skinned and slashed chicken thighs. Roast at 190°C (375°F) Gas Mark 5 for 35–45 minutes. Steam the couscous as above in stock. Stir in the remaining oil and lemon juice. Add 4 finely chopped spring onions, 3 tablespoons chopped mint, 3 tablespoons chopped parsley and 2 chopped tomatoes. Spoon on to plates, top with the chicken and serve with lemon wedges.
Calories per serving 440

citrus chicken with rice salad

Calories per serving **499**
Serves **2**
Preparation time **10 minutes,**
    plus marinating
Cooking time **15 minutes**

2 boneless, skinless **chicken
    breasts**, sliced lengthways
    into strips
2 tablespoons **buttermilk**
grated rind and juice of ½ **lime**
1 **garlic clove**, crushed

Rice salad
100 g (3½ oz) **mixed basmati
    and wild rice**
1 tablespoon **olive oil**
4 **spring onions**, sliced
25 g (1 oz) **cashew nuts**,
    roughly chopped
handful of **baby leaf spinach**
grated rind and juice of
    1 **orange**
1 tablespoon **soy sauce**

Put the chicken strips in a non-metallic dish. Mix together the buttermilk, lime rind and juice and garlic, pour the mixture over the chicken, turn to coat evenly and set aside for at least 10 minutes. Alternatively, prepare the marinade in the morning and leave the chicken in it in the refrigerator all day.

Cook the rice according to the instructions on the packet. Drain thoroughly.

Heat the oil in a small frying pan. Fry the spring onions for 1 minute. Toss the spring onions through the rice, and then add the cashew nuts, spinach, orange rind and juice and soy sauce. Set aside.

Thread the chicken evenly on 4 skewers and cook, turning from time to time, under a preheated hot grill for 4–5 minutes. Serve with the rice salad.

For coleslaw, as a accompanimanet to replace rice salad, finely shred ¼ each of white and red cabbage and 1 carrot. Finely slice ½ red onion and mix everything together in a bowl with 1 tablespoon roughly chopped parsley. To make the dressing whisk 150 ml (¼ pint) reduced-fat mayonnaise, ½ tablespoon white wine vinegar and a pinch of caster sugar and season with salt and pepper. Toss the dressing through the cabbage mixture and leave to stand for at least 30 minutes before serving. **Calories per serving 430**

chicken, okra & red lentil dhal

Calories per serving **499**
Serves **4**
Preparation time **15 minutes**
Cooking time **45 minutes**

2 teaspoons **ground cumin**
1 teaspoon **ground coriander**
½ teaspoon **cayenne pepper**
¼ teaspoon **ground turmeric**
500 g (1 lb) boneless, skinless **chicken thighs**, cut into large pieces
3 tablespoons **oil**
1 **onion**, sliced
2 **garlic cloves**, crushed
25 g (1 oz) **fresh root ginger**, finely chopped
750 ml (1¼ pints) **water**
300 g (10 oz) **red lentils**, rinsed
200 g (7 oz) **okra**
small handful of **fresh coriander**, chopped
salt

To serve
lime wedges

Mix together the cumin, coriander, cayenne and turmeric and toss with the chicken pieces.

Heat the oil in a large saucepan. Fry the chicken pieces in batches until deep golden, draining each batch to a plate. Add the onion to the pan and fry for 5 minutes until browned. Stir in the garlic and ginger and cook for a further 1 minute.

Return the chicken to the pan and add the measurement water. Bring to the boil, then reduce the heat and simmer very gently, covered, for 20 minutes until the chicken is cooked through. Add the lentils and cook for 5 minutes. Stir in the okra, coriander and a little salt and cook for a further 5 minutes until the lentils are tender but not completely pulpy.

Check the seasoning and serve in shallow bowls with the lime wedges.

For chicken, courgette & chilli dhal, use 200 g (7 oz) courgettes, thinly sliced, instead of the okra. For a hotter flavour, add a thinly sliced medium-strength red chilli with the garlic and ginger. **Calories per serving 495**

230

chicken wrapped in parma ham

Calories per serving **324**
Serves **4**
Preparation time **10 minutes**
Cooking time **10 minutes**

4 boneless, skinless **chicken breasts**, about 150 g (5 oz) each
4 slices of **Parma ham**
4 **sage leaves**
plain flour, for dusting
25 g (1 oz) **butter**
2 tablespoons **olive oil**
4 sprigs **cherry tomatoes on the vine**
150 ml (½ pint) **dry white wine**
salt and **pepper**
green salad, to serve

Lay each chicken breast between 2 sheets of clingfilm and flatten with a rolling pin or meat mallet until wafer thin. Season with salt and pepper.

Wrap a slice of Parma ham around each chicken breast, followed by a sage leaf. Secure the sage and ham in position with a cocktail stick, then lightly dust both sides of the chicken with flour. Season again with salt and pepper.

Heat the butter and oil in a large frying pan over a high heat, add the chicken and cook for 4–5 minutes on each side or until the juices run clear when pierced with a knife. Add the tomatoes and wine to the pan and bubble until the wine has thickened and reduced by about half. Serve immediately, with a green salad.

For chicken escalopes with rosemary & pancetta,

take 4 chicken breasts, about 200 g (4 oz) each, and flatten as above. Top each flattened escalope with a scattering of rosemary leaves, then wrap each in a slice of pancetta, instead of the Parma ham (omit the sage). Dust with flour, season with salt and pepper and cook as above. **Calories per serving 335**

chicken with red wine & grapes

Calories per serving **368**
Serves **4**
Preparation time **5 minutes**
Cooking time **30 minutes**

3 tablespoons **olive oil**
4 **boneless, skinless chicken breasts**, about 150 g (5 oz) each
1 **red onion**, sliced
2 tablespoons **red pesto** (see below for homemade)
300 ml (½ pint) **red wine**
300 ml (½ pint) **water**
125 g (4 oz) **red grapes**, halved and deseeded
salt and **black pepper**
basil leaves, to garnish

Heat 2 tablespoons of the oil in a large frying pan, add the chicken breasts and cook over a medium heat for 5 minutes, turning frequently, until browned all over. Remove from the pan with a slotted spoon and drain on kitchen paper.

Heat the remaining oil in the pan, add the onion slices and pesto and cook, stirring constantly, for 3 minutes until the onion is softened but not browned.

Add the wine and measurement water to the pan and bring to the boil. Return the chicken breasts to the pan and season with salt and pepper to taste. Reduce the heat and simmer for 15 minutes, or until the chicken is cooked through.

Stir in the grapes and serve immediately, garnished with basil leaves.

For homemade red pesto, put 1 chopped garlic clove, ½ teaspoon sea salt, 25 g (1 oz) basil leaves, 50 g (2 oz) drained sun-dried tomatoes in oil, 125 ml (4 fl oz) extra virgin olive oil and a little pepper in a food processor or blender and blend until smooth. Transfer to a bowl and stir in 2 tablespoons freshly grated Parmesan cheese. **Calories per serving 368**

index

acknowledgements

Commissioning editor: Eleanor Maxfield
Designer: Jeremy Tilston
Editor: Pauline Bache
Production controller: Sarah Kramer

Octopus Publishing Group 65, 73; David Loftus 9, 175, 213; David Munns 1, 11, 14, 15, 16, 17, 23, 27, 61, 71, 89, 91, 97, 101, 127, 129, 147, 151, 155, 165, 189, 203, 217; Gareth Sambidge 235; Ian Wallace 18, 36, 67, 99, 166, 221, 227; Lis Parsons 2, 25, 33, 35, 41, 103, 105, 135, 137, 139, 145, 153, 171, 179, 181, 187, 191, 195, 197, 199, 215, 223, 225, 231; Peter Myers 55; Sean Myers 4, 29, 43, 49, 133, 169, 193; Stephen Conroy 6, 8, 51, 83, 92, 109, 115, 131, 141, 157, 173, 183, 185, 205, 207, 209, 211, 229, 233; Will Heap 12, 31, 69, 75, 77, 81, 95, 111, 113, 119, 121, 123, 125, 149, 159; William Lingwood 59, 63, 143; William Reavell 57, 79, 87, 117; William Shaw 10, 13, 21, 39, 45, 47, 53, 85, 107, 161, 163, 177, 201, 219.